CW00350081

Once Bitten

by

NIGEL VARDY

Book Design and Setting by **Neil Coe**
(neil@cartadesign.co.uk)

Set in Rotis Serif 11pt on 14pt

First published in 2008 by;

Ecademy Press

6 Woodland Rise, Penryn,
Cornwall UK TR10 8QD
info@ecademy-press.com
www.ecademy-press.com

Printed and Bound by;
Lightning Source in the UK and USA

Printed on acid-free paper from managed forests. This book
is printed on demand, so no copies will be remaindered or
pulped.

ISBN 978-1-905823-27-7

*The rights of the persons named in the title of each chapter to be identified
as the authors of this work has been asserted in accordance with sections
77 and 78 of the Copyright Designs and Patents Act 1988.*

A CIP catalogue record for this book is available from the British Library.

*All rights reserved. No part of this publication may be reproduced in
any material form (including photocopying or storing in any medium
by electronic means and whether or not transiently or incidentally to
some other use of this publication) without the written permission of the
copyright holder except in accordance with the provisions of the Copyright,
Designs and Patents Act 1988. Applications for the Copyright holders
written permission to reproduce any part of this publication should be
addressed to the publishers.*

CONTENTS

GLOSSARY

Belay – The securing of a rope on rock or ice during climbing.

Bergschrund – A crevasse or series of crevasses, usually deep and often broad, occurring near the head of a mountain glacier

Couloir – A deep mountainside gorge or gully

Crevasse – A deep open chasm in a glacier

DENSAN – Our expedition name (Short for Denali, Steve, Anthony & Nigel)

Down Climbing – The opposite of climbing up!

Front Pointing – Standing on the front points of crampons especially when climbing steep slopes

Jumar – A mechanical device for ascending a rope

Karabiner – An oblong metal ring with a spring clip, often used to attach a running rope to a climber or their equipment.

PTT Switch – Press to Talk switch on a two way radio

Spindrift – Small ice particles usually flying in the wind

White Gas – A type of liquid fuel for mountain stoves

Windslab – Layers of snow deposited by the wind

MAP OF McKINLEY

ACKNOWLEDGEMENTS

I would like to thank the following people for their support...

Steve Ball and Antony Hollinshead my fellow climbers without whom I couldn't have survived the mountain, all the staff at Providence Medical Centre Alaska for all their help, Diddy Hitchens for being a complete star! The Denali National Parks Department and Rescue Services for saving my life, Malcolm and Karen Daly for being there for me in Alaska, Patrick Minder for supporting Amanda and me in Alaska, everyone at Nottingham City Hospital for rebuilding my life and keeping me climbing, Nicky Cockerill (nee Bentley) for her friendship and physio skills, my Mum and Dad for being there (and putting up with me for this long), my big sister Amanda and her family for keeping me above water and supporting my exploits, Jamie and Clare Glazebrook for being great friends and supporting me, Richard Bull for making me laugh and bringing in the beer, Chris Chadwick for all his drive and enlightenment, Bob Forbes for his patience and enthusiasm, Ian and Jean Henderson for climbing and drinking with me all these years, everyone at Terra Nova Ltd for their support, Steve Pountain for helping me shoot again, Rob Edmonds for all his help at getting boots to fit me, Martin Moran for getting me back into the mountains, Chris Dale for taking me on some epic technical climbs and David Broom for pushing me on the big routes.

And finally...

Mindy Gibbins-Klein for all her help in writing and producing this book and Tina Moult for giving me the drive (and the kick up the bum) to get it finished!

INTRODUCTION BY THE AUTHOR

I entered this world at 10pm on a wet and windy night in 1969 and weighed in at a mighty 10lb 1oz - natural. It is a fact my mother has never let me forget. I was the only boy born on the ward that week and had a fearsome grip and bellowing lungs.

The swinging sixties were almost at a close. In the few months left Man walked on the Moon, Woodstock brought music to the world and Derby County were promoted to Division One.

I had a wonderful childhood and was brought up by two loving parents. I was allowed to play in the woods, pinch fruit and vegetables from the garden and build dens galore. I made few friends but had an active imagination which kept me happy for hours.

Parallel to my childhood life was another, that of my older sister. By the time I was eight or nine she was banging her head away to heavy metal and causing the usual early teenage hell. At first I couldn't understand what it was all but within a few years her influences had been passed down and I began my lifelong addiction to bands such as Queen and Led Zeppelin. I became a DJ at thirteen and turned the 'wheels of steel' until my late twenties.

Most people wouldn't own up to being a swat at school but I'm afraid I'll have to. I was both a Prefect and a Librarian. I always did my homework on time and it took a real illness to keep me away from the classroom. My mind was transfixed by Chemistry and Physics, as I loved experimenting. I regularly mixed everything together at the end of the chemistry lesson hoping for some excitement – a fizz or perhaps a bang but alas nothing ever happened. I electrocuted a few people in Physics though!

My teens were faced with darker moments. It was the depression of the 1980's and my Dad worked in the steel industry. Times were hard and he found himself unemployed for the first time in his life. I watched him sit in disbelief and depression as the world went by. No one wanted his skills and he felt abandoned. With little help he picked himself up from the doldrums and became a self-employed Decorator until he retired. My Mum has worked in everything from hosiery to cleaning, finally becoming a home help. Between them they worked very hard to bring up my sister and I the best way they could.

I was in my teens when outdoor pursuits were part of the school curriculum and a part of my life. Unfortunately climbing and abseiling scared me witless as I suffered severe vertigo. I still hate looking over a cliff edge to this day. People may find this a strange truth for someone who climbs but it is perfectly true. I find snow a much easier medium to look over as it disguises the actual angle of the drop (well, it does for me). I preferred to sail and spent many a happy hour tacking up and down the local reservoirs getting cold and wet.

I left school in 1985 with five 'o' levels and three cse's and began my ascent into the world of electrical engineering. At sixteen I started an apprenticeship at the Electricity Board, rising to Engineer by my early twenties.

But where did the adventure part of me come from? There were no other travellers in my family. Holidays were spent at the seaside and weekends in the garden or walking in Derbyshire. I can only put it down to my father's interest in Warfare. Many children of my generation built model kits, played with toy soldiers and read about the adventures of armies overseas. I was fascinated by the battles of World War II and read of places such as El Alamein, Rangoon and Singapore. I scanned the pages of the family atlas to find these far off places and I dreamed. I wanted to see them with my own eyes and imagine history. It was all a bit Boys Own but I loved it.

In 1994 I went on a Raleigh International expedition to Chile. It was here that my real adventures began. Three months of rain, community work, rain, trekking, rain, plate tectonics and occasional rain turned me into an all-English adventurer. I took a Union Flag everywhere and probably drove everyone wild. By now I had a niece and two nephews who gave me the title of "Uncle travelling Nigel". To this day it has stuck to me like glue.

People who know me well say that I was born a century too late. I should have been an explorer in the age of Scott or Shackleton and travelled across the world in the quest for adventure. Unfortunately those days are gone. The world has been mapped from space and almost every corner explored, well almost...

I started climbing in my twenties and after a summer on the rock, I began a winter on ice and snow. Something inside me began to change. Though I enjoyed rock I still held my childhood fear of heights, yet on the ice I wasn't too bothered. To this day I don't know why it is, only that it is. As a child I had always preferred the snows of winter as the heat of summer brought on severe catarrh. Perhaps my subconscious was talking to me? I made for Snowdonia, the Lake District or the Highlands of Scotland when I could and loved every minute. Work kept me busy but climbing became a major part of my life.

My climbing got higher and harder and I needed new challenges. I passed the 20,000ft mark in the mountains of Bolivia, before sitting down to dinner one evening with a group of friends. After only a few minutes a life-changing question was asked. "Do you fancy a trip to Alaska next year?" A new adventure was about to begin.

SECTION 1
THE STORY

Writing this book has brought back to me vivid memories of May 1999. That pivotal month changed my life forever. One moment I was a 30 year old climber, the next a hospital case. What follows is the story of what happened to me and how I lived through it. I'll let you to read the rest and say only this.

"I don't want to die in an unused body"

Anon

Flying over the Alaska Range

CHAPTER 1
APPROACH

"There's the Alaskan Alps Guys!" screamed the pilot. He pointed vigorously towards a cluster of small jagged peaks down to our left. The din of the engine was overpowering and I struggled to hear him through the aged headphones strapped to my head. I peered over the nosecone and noticed a clutch of peaks dwarfed by the monsters of the Alaska Range which surrounded us with their towers of ice and snow, stretching as far as the eye could see. In moments they were gone. Only half an hour ago we had left the sugar-coated pines of Talkeetna behind us and now we were dodging the mountain tops heading for the Kahiltna Glacier. I was wedged in the co-pilots seat of a four-seat Cessna ski plane and my feet were pushing my knees up almost into my chin. I rattled from top to bottom as the plane buffeted along and before me dials galore confused my eyes with their needles whizzing round. Behind me were Steve and Ant, crammed side by side into the tail section with the climbing gear and supplies. "How's it going lads?" I shouted, but there was no reply. They were busy staring out of the windows and anyway, it was too loud to hear me. I turned back to do some staring myself but inside I felt tired and queasy. I'd suffered a long night lying in my bunk. Jetlag kept me awake and I'd coughed the house down from my dry, wheezy chest. I'd thrown some tablets down my throat and managed a few hours precious sleep before I had to force myself out of bed. I had risen early to take my last shower, knowing that on my return the classic climbing odour of stale sweat and caked on food would have taken its hold.

Suddenly the mountains parted and below us lay the Kahiltna Glacier. Burning sunlight beamed up from the snow but in the distance I could just make out a small cluster of dots on the ice. It was base camp. The pilot threw the stick forward and right and swooped down at a near vertical angle for the runway. I hate flying in these little cans and detest landing but I wasn't going to admit it. I gripped the seat and clenched my teeth. 'Some bloody climber I am,' I thought. The plane levelled off and we began our approach onto the ice. Outside it was a near perfect day and I noticed a lonely windsock flapping in the breeze. Seconds later we hit the ice with a reassuring bump, shot up the slope, did a handbrake turn and stopped. "Here we are guys, it's all yours," the pilot said comically. The roller coaster ride was over. To him this was just a normal day in the office.

I pulled the door open to be hit with the fresh, biting cold mountain air. My cheeks tightened and my breath clouded as I jumped out onto the iron like ice. "Thank God that's over", I whispered. I was a bit shaken, but not stirred. I knew the flight home would do the same to me but that was weeks away and my mind had more important things to consider. Steve and Ant bundled themselves out and began tossing kit out onto the ice. There were 120lbs of food, tents, climbing gear and equipment for each of us to carry. From this moment on we had to be self-sufficient until our return to the town of Talkeetna, three weeks climbing and forty minutes flight time away.

In the corner of my eye I noticed a little bundled figure bounding down the slope towards us. She waved her arms with joy and screamed "Hi guys! I'm Annie; I'm the ranger here. Welcome to Camp!" She was based on the glacier to register climbing groups on and off the range and was always glad to see a few new faces. Her face was deeply tanned but I could see little else of her under all the layers of fleece and down. What did shine out was her personality. She was a bundle of fun and obviously loved being on camp. She lived in a plastic cabin just off the runway with a view out the front door to die for. Mts. Foraker and Hunter stared right in her face. They soared above the glacier with a perfect blue sky to silhouette them against the snow.

The air was now silent save for the distant buzz of the Cessna and Annie said, "There's a good camping spot already dug out if you want it." Before any of us could get a word in she was tearing off up the slope to our prospective home for the night. We dragged the bags up the snow to a large flat terrace which had been dug deep into the snowy bank. "It only wants a bit of tidying up lads and we're in," said Steve in a happy voice. A dump of fresh snow had recently fallen making it an easy job to square off the walls and make our nightly home. We had more gear to come but it was delayed until late afternoon, so we pitched the tents and set about cutting ice blocks to build a wall around camp. The weather in the Alaska Range can be fierce. Winds in excess of 100mph and storms lasting for days at a time are not uncommon, even at base camp. If you leave your tent exposed in such conditions the wind will pick it up and roll it down the glacier, complete with you and all your kit in it. It would be like watching a paper bag blow around a field.

I walked down towards Annie's hut and grabbed four gallons of white gas and three sledges. I had never towed a sledge before as on my previous climbing exploits we had used porters. Up here, you're on your own - what you take, you carry. This is what makes McKinley such an epic challenge. Steve loaded his kitbag onto a sledge, roped it onto his harness and tried a pull. After only a few feet it had rolled over, tumbled down the slope and dragged him staggering behind it. Ant and myself sniggered like a couple of school lads. We tried the same and Steve had his laugh. There is nothing worse than looking like a bunch of idiots before a group of people, particularly climbers. You are supposed to know exactly what you are doing at all times and look calm and collected. Bravado can soon take over. A few choice words were said but after a couple of hours we had mastered the art of sledge pulling. One thing did worry me though. I'd heard horror stories of sledge pulling on McKinley. It was the one thing you never forgot. The constant drag of it behind you and the fear of falling into a crevasse with it dragging you down niggled at the back of my mind but there was nothing I could do about it.

The camp was up, kit was packed and there was nothing to do. Boredom began to creep in. "I could take a wander around camp and see who else is here," I thought to myself. I grabbed my cup of tea and stood up straight to scan the clusters of stationary tents. The scene was reminiscent of the trenches in World War I. Shelters were dug deep into the snow and equipment was lying around drying under the sun. The few people who were around dodged the cold shadows and ran from tent to tent. I hardly said a word to anyone and wandered along with my thoughts.

Shade began to cloak the valley and I felt the cold begin to bite. I walked back to camp, pulled on my down jacket and got inside the tent. The stoves were roaring away as Ant boiled pans of water for a brew. I always find the sound of a stove reassuring. If you can brew up then all is usually fine with the world and it is almost physically impossible to drink too much tea, coffee and hot chocolate when you're on a mountain. Ant rattled the cooking pans and served up our first meal of the trip. Mashed potato, beef jerky and a special Ant sauce. It was marvellous. When everything around you is frozen solid, the warm feeling that food gives you inside is a dream. Ant had a large bag of spices hidden away in the gear and he intended to use a good dose of them in every meal. Expedition food has the reputation of being very dull, but not with Ant. He was an excellent and imaginative cook. With every bite I could feel my throat tingle but the aftertaste kept me burping all evening.

Within the hour we had eaten up, cleaned up, and were huddled inside our sleeping bags trying to keep what little warmth we had inside us. "Don't worry lads, I'll keep you warm" cried Ant. I looked across to his tent and saw an outstretched hand clutching a bottle of whisky. "Here, try a spot of this!" Ever since I had known Ant he had always been a bit of a lad and as ever he had come prepared. Drinking alcohol in the cold doesn't warm you up at all but the bravado between the three of us had got its way and we all threw a large dram down our throats. I felt it burn reassuringly as it sank into my stomach and I coughed like a barking hound. My throat was still sore.

I laid back and stared up at the tent roof. I breathed out and watched the cloud of mist turn into millions of tiny ice crystals. They were stationary for only a moment before I felt them rain cold down on my face and melt into my skin. We were here at last. The months of planning and training had ended and tomorrow we would be off up the glacier to begin the long drag to McKinley - kit, sledges and all. Inside I felt relaxed, happy and cold. The adventure had begun.

My eyes burst open in the early hours. I needed the toilet and I needed it now! I tried to ignore the impending pain of my overanxious bladder, but it was no good. I hadn't got a piss bottle in the tent yet, so I forced myself out of my bag and sprinted down the glacier to the toilet. The rangers have built permanent ones on camp to prevent contamination of the ice and they insist you use them. It was so cold that my piss froze as it hit the ground and my hands fumbled at the zip with a numbing throb as I tried to pull it closed. "Come on, work you little bastards!" I mumbled as I forced my fingers to respond. They had only been exposed for a few seconds but it had been enough to numb them to the bone. I ran back to the tent and buried myself inside my bag in an attempt to warm up. When I eventually got up at 7.30am, I looked at the thermometer on my watch, it was still -15C in the tent. I dreaded to think what it had been earlier. My feet were cold and I was shivering. I reached out to open the tent zip and was instantly hit by a shower of ice, which rained down from the roof. "Bloody hell!" I cried. Tiny crystals ran across my neck and began to melt down my spine. It wasn't a good start to the day.

Soon the stoves were roaring but the water took an age

to boil. A single pan needed almost an hour to turn from its freezing state to bubbling. I could feel an unsaid air of concern rise over the camp. Ant looked out from his tent door "We'd better take another can of fuel up top I think, "he said. Steve and I agreed. It would be extra weigh, but we needed it.

We left camp and descended the gentle slope of Heartbreak Hill, before turning right and moving up onto the main flow of the Kahiltna. The sledge began banging into my heels with an incessant tap, tap, tap. I tried re-setting the ropes but no matter what I did the tapping returned. It didn't take long to get me really wound up but by the time I had sorted out the knots we had walked to the bottom of the slope and were pulling uphill on the Kahiltna. Sanity returned. Before us a beautifully carved path was running right up the centre of the ice, weaving only here and there where a crevasse blocked the straight route.

The sun beat down on us with a vengeance and sweat ran down my back. I looked at Steve. He was still in his fleece jacket. "It keeps the sun off the back of my neck" was his reason but it would have killed me to wear mine. It must have reached over 30C on the exposed glacier and I plastered enough sun cream on my face to resemble the entire Aussie Cricket Team. It felt cool against my skin but it blocked the pores and just made the sweating worse than ever. I was carrying 60lb on my back and towing the same on my sledge. My shoulders felt ok under the rucksacks weight but my waist felt sore round the edges of my hips with the sledge's incessant pulling. As soon as you stopped walking, the sledge would drift back downhill but at least it didn't pull you backward too hard and it was easy enough to start again.

After a couple of hours we stopped for a brew and took a break. When you are fully concentrating on what you are doing, where every foot is going, getting your breathing right and keeping body and soul together, you forget who and what is around you. We hadn't talked much except for a few shouts here and there. Being tied 30 feet apart and roped together doesn't do much for conversation. I sat down on my rucksack and stared in awe at the size of the surrounding peaks which were almost exclusively white from top to bottom, save the occasional rocky outcrop sticking out from the ice. They looked close enough to touch but they were over a mile away. The glacier seemed a never-ending expanse of icy desert, barren and empty but for the now distant drone of a plane descending to base camp, or the odd climbing party slogging up the plateau. I find a great deal of inner peace when I'm in these surroundings and all of work's stresses and strains seem to melt away in the silent snows. " The boss can do what the hell he likes now, I don't care a toss," I thought to myself. It is pitiful that it takes a place such as this to let me clear my thoughts and empty my mind. I got so involved with my work most of the time that everything else got blanked out. Relationships, family, friends, all seemed to suffer because of my job. It's a lame excuse I know but work had been much of my life for the past 14 years. Only climbing and expeditions had ever kept me sane.

Steve led the rope, Ant brought up the rear and I was sandwiched in the middle. After only a few hours on the ice I had noticed the two very different attitudes between them. Steve was the leader, ready to try anything and lead by example. Ant was happy just plodding along making sure everyone was ok and playing Tail End Charlie. I was happy to do either and everyone seemed happy enough. It was 7pm before we reached the cut off for the Kahiltna North east Fork (or Death Valley) and built our Camp 1.

Most climbers tend to attempt the Washburn Route and camp here before continuing up the ice for another mile or so but we were keeping well away from the commercial enterprises and heading for the hopefully peaceful West Rib. There was no luxury of an empty hole to pitch our tents this time, so we grabbed the shovels and set about the snows with a vengeance. For years I had worked on road gangs smashing up tarmac and concrete, so shifting the soft snow was a joy. I paced out the hole to be about 15 feet square and 4 feet deep. We piled a good wall around the edges and got on with the domestic side of climbing – food! I was aching for a cup of tea and a bite to eat.

I hadn't long finished scraping the last morsels of food from my pot when I glanced down at my watch and noticed the time – it was five to eight. "Who's got the radio?" I asked. "It's nearly time for Annie's weather forecast". There was a rustle from behind me and out popped the handset. The Air Taxi office in Talkeetna had supplied us with the only means of contact with the outside world. I had been in the mountains many times before and never had communication with base but just consider your position. If anything goes wrong with the radio - that's it. There's no mobile phone or calling for help out here. No voice in the outside world to talk to – nothing – no one. This little piece of kit was of paramount importance to us all.

Climbers know the effect the weather can have on them – it can mean the difference between a summit attempt or not, a life or a death. I turned on the handset and through the crackles came Annie's distant voice. Tomorrow would be cloudy, warm and quite bearable but we would be in crevasse country and visibility would be everything. Walking under a white sky against a white floor full of white crevasses would be difficult if not impossible. I forced my way out of the tent door and stood outside staring down the glacier. I sipped away at a cup of steaming tea and contemplated the day. We had worked well together and pulled all our gear up to camp 1. I glanced at my watch and was shocked to see it was 10.30pm. The light evening had fooled me into thinking that it was much earlier. I was still used to the sunset times back home but we were much further north now and darkness hardly fell. It only took a dim light to fall onto the ice to make it seem like the daylight I was used to. I slurped down the last dregs from my cup, tossed it inside the tent porch and eased my stiff body into my sleeping bag.

After the exertions of yesterday, we got up late. The sledge towing had taken its toll on our backs and muscles. I reached out a cold hand and suddenly stopped myself. I remembered what would happen the minute I rattled the tent – the morning ice shower would come! I carefully pulled everything away from the tent door before daring to touch the zip. With a gentle ease I slowly pulled it back and spilled not one crystal. Outside it was bright and cold with very little wind - a perfect morning but I could feel a dull ache inside my head. I still had a terrible cold and threw down a couple of headache tablets to help numb the pain. Packing up the camp warmed me up bodily but my hands were suffering badly. I hadn't felt the cold like this at such a low altitude before. 63 degrees north (the Arctic Circle is 66.5 degrees north) makes the summers bright but cold and height for height, McKinley is colder than Everest.

A ghostly cloud began to roll silently out of Death Valley but occasionally the West Rib broke through. It was a four-mile pull to get to the base and we had managed over seven the day before. The map showed dense crevasse fields but with a little skill and patience they could be overcome. In Talkeetna, the Rangers had briefed us about the dangers of Death Valley. It was renowned for avalanches but this year we were lucky. Snow had not built up on the cliffs and we were about to be the first people in two years to enter it. Imagine that. There are few places left in the world where no foot has trodden for so long. The last century has seen man extend his grasp on the world and hardly a place is left where we don't go but imagine being that first man. It would be like casting your eyes on a lost Amazonian city or some untouched jungle. It would be clean, perfect and untouched.

We left camp and began the drag into Death Valley. There were no tracks to guide us now, no footprints to follow. Today's success or failure was going to be down to good navigation, skill and old-fashioned luck. This time I led but with no bag to weigh me down - just snowshoes and walking poles. It was my job to spot the crevasses, find a safe way through them and guide the lads as they followed on behind me. Steve took the middle of the rope and once again Ant brought up the rear. After quickly covering the flat ground, a frozen labyrinth reared its ugly head before me. Deep down the ice was breaking itself apart with enormous pressure and bringing to the surface the fractures it created - crevasses. My eyes flashed from left to right as I mapped in my mind the best way through the maze. It looked an awesome undertaking to find a way through but I wound my way through the first sections with some success. We crossed a large ice bridge but behind us the cloud was forming high in the valley and tumbling downward. The visibility dropped in minutes and I felt exhausted from the incessant start stop of crevasse navigation. The temperature fell dramatically and ice crystals began to glitter through the air.

We were forced to make camp. Despite our hardest efforts we had only covered three miles all day but we had gained some height and distance. It's easy to be self critical in situations like this and at that I was expert. Annie's voice rang out at 8pm with tomorrows forecast. Light winds, snow showers and mild temperatures.

I walked a few feet away from camp, stared blankly into the distance and closed my eyes. A slow shiver ran up my spine but it wasn't from the cold - an inner peace was filling up my soul. I felt strangely alone and in a perfect environment - no litter, no smells, and no noise, just me. I was rid of the world of mobile phones, pagers, five o'clock deadlines and traffic jams.

The months of pollution were clearing from my lungs in the clean, cold air. It was a wonderful moment. "Tea's up Nige!" shouted Ant. The moment was lost but not forgotten.

A dull rumbling woke me in the night. I prised my eyes apart and whilst my mind considered whether I was dreaming or asleep it dawned on me what was going on – it was an avalanche! I jumped up but I soon realised that it was a long way up the valley and anyway, if it were going to engulf me, it would have already done it. The tons of ice and snow thudded along for a few moments and silence reigned again.

The next time I opened my eyes the tent was illuminated with bright sunlight and the air felt warm. I stuck my hand outside to find soft powdery snow falling silently to the ground. Cocooned in my downy bag, I felt little like getting up, but we had to climb. Last night we had decided to go back down to camp 1 today and bring up all the supplies we had left behind. This was going to be not only a technical climb but also a logistical one. Supplies had to be ferried up and down the route whilst still wanting to make the summit and be back home in three and a half weeks.

In just over an hour we were back down at camp 1, a journey which yesterday had taken seven. A few scattered tents had taken up residence but they were deserted. Tracks lay in lines heading up the glacier but one set had left the motorway and followed ours. An American team were joining us on the West Rib. Their progress was slow but they were carrying over thirty days worth of food and supplies. We had met them briefly at base camp and already seemed like old friends.

We hauled our way back to camp 2 laden with all we needed, leaving the rest for our return. We soon approached the American's Camp and saw a ghostly figure shaking a thermos flask. Tony, Steve, Geoff and Barbara fed us hot juice and talked of routes, crevasses and radios. They had flattened their batteries by leaving the set on by mistake one evening. They

Camp 2 Kahiltna NE Fork

The West Rib

Negotiating the Icefall

Steve, Myself & Ant

could receive no weather reports or advise base camp of their position so we agreed to give Annie a shout later and to keep in touch when we could. They seemed an experienced team and looked hardened climbers. All the men wore thick beards and beaming smiles while Barbara wore a bronze tan and had deep brown hair which flicked in the wind. We joked about the weather and drank more juice before saying our goodbyes and heading off to camp.

That evening the suns shadow fell across the valley with eclipse like speed. The temperature fell similarly but my face was still burning from the heat of the sun. I plastered on thick cream every day but the UV was still getting through. My nose stung and both my earlobes were peeling.

The next morning was bitter cold and we lay in until the sun warmed the tent. It was just too cold to bear. We buried half the food and fuel and set off for camp 3. As usual, Steve led with me in the middle and Ant bringing up the rear. Armed with snowshoes, Steve crossed the snow bridges and navigated our path. The warm sunshine was softening the ice, making the bridges a serious problem but with great care Steve straddled the cracks and shouted their position back.

I approached an unassuming looking depression in the snow, strode over the crack and shifted my bodyweight forward. Suddenly I flew forward, dropping onto the floor out of control. Before I had time to scream, I had sunk up to my armpits. My feet flayed around, but there was nothing below me but emptiness. A silence filled the air and everything seemed still. I opened my eyes and looked out only inches above the floor. My arms were stuck out sideways and ice was pushing hard into my armpits. I caught my breath and realised what had happened. I was up to my chest in a crevasse and jammed tight by my rucksack. I felt the sledge give a dull thud as it tapped against my back. My heart was racing at breakneck speed and my lungs pumped air frantically. "Think about what you're doing Nigel", I nervously thought to myself "calm down for Gods sake or you'll never get out!" Neither Steve nor Ant could help as they were holding the rope tight to stop me going down any further. I was on my own. I threw my feet out looking for the icy walls of the crevasse. Both crampons bit into good ice and with a gentle push, they took my weight. Thank God I had got my crampons on. My ski poles flapped uselessly as I tried to get a purchase on the snow above. They were a hindrance still strapped to my wrists, so I ripped them off and flung them away. Slowly I stood up and rolled forward onto the snow. I gave a deep breath and smiled. I was safe. I began to laugh but I don't know why. I had hardly cheated death by any means but my nerves just lost control and I howled. I fell twice more that afternoon, and laughed every time.

The ground began to steepen as we approached the head of the valley. Before us stood the Icefall. It is a well-known landmark and stories abound of its difficulties. Many climbers suffer nightmare journeys through this short section of ice and straight away we could see why. We had to rig pulleys to drag the sledge and fought for every foot of ground. Pressure ridges towered ice 40ft above our heads and navigating a path between them seemed almost impossible. We just kept coming up against dead ends. Tension began to rise as time went by and eventually we camped in the maze. It was a precarious place to stay the night but we had little choice. Steve buried all the snow stakes and ice screws we had and roped the tent up. Ant and I started digging. The snow soon gave way to ice and axes replaced shovels. I broke into a crevasse at one point and we had to move camp. A magenta sunset flooded the valley ending the day, which seemed the only conciliation for our work. I skulked into the tent and dug out a bottle of whisky. We toasted the day in a somewhat uneasy mood and closed up shop for the night.

The uneven floor pushed into my back but I didn't care, I was so tired I could have slept on a clothesline and within minutes

I was gone.

Next morning the sun was high in the sky but the Cassin Ridge leered its shadow over our tents and it was still icy cold. In the distance I saw four dots approaching our last camp. The American Team was catching up. All they had to do was keep following our tracks and although nothing was said at the time I could feel the air of a race had begun.

Steve and Ant looked over the horizon to find a path through the maze. Before us lay a tremendous crevasse with no obvious way round. "Nothing for it lads, we'll just have to go through it," said Steve confidently. We tried setting up a pulley for the bags but it was no good. Instead they were dragged down by hand whilst I climbed out the other side. I smashed my crampons into the ice but they had little effect. My axes did little better. The ice was as hard as iron and brittle as glass. Halfway up I tried to get an ice screw into the wall but it just sheared it away. 'Sod it' I thought, 'I'll just have to risk it'. Blow after blow I plodded my axes and crampons up the face sending shattered ice down onto Ant and Steve. I threw an arm over the top and buried my axe shaft into the snow above. I was safe. In quick procession Steve and Ant followed me, but it had taken over an hour to travel just 100yds.

Eventually we pulled into camp 3. It was late in the evening and the sun was fading. I was starving. Dried food isn't usually appetising but with a little flair Ant cooked up a delicious meal of minute rice and reindeer jerky. Your food goes from piping hot to stone cold in minutes, so manners are minimal. I could have eaten loads more but you have to balance weight with volume. What you carry you can take. Fortunately I had feasted for the last few weeks before coming out and put half a stone on but already it was vanishing fast.

Annie's voice brought us a changing forecast with stiffening winds and snow showers on the cards. We were now over 11,000ft above sea level and the first twinges of altitude were beginning to bite.

CHAPTER 2
GAINING HEIGHT

Beep beep beep! Shouted my watch. I eased a hand from inside my sleeping bag and scratched the ice from its face. It was 6.45am and bitterly cold. The inside of the tent was white over and icy crystals hung over my head ready to shower down at the slightest disturbance. Steve groaned a lazy "good morning" before turning over and burying his head deep inside his sleeping bag. The first real climbing was about to begin and I should have been bursting from my bed full of energy but I felt little like getting up. It had been a long and uncomfortable night. My back ached from top to bottom and my feet were freezing cold. I carefully opened the tent and lit the stove in the porch. My hand was only was exposed for a few seconds but it froze numb and I had to pull it deep into my bag to re-warm it. Little heat could be felt from the stove's flames and the small pot of ice took an age to melt. It was almost an hour before it boiled enough for a brew. With a ruffle of flying ice and nylon Ant's head peered from inside his tent, "hello chaps" he bellowed in his best smooth talking voice. At least he sounded happy, which was much better than I felt. All I wanted to do was crawl back into bed and sleep for a week.

We reached the base of the climb at about 1pm. I was disgusted by our slow progress. Though the daylight was plentiful, we needed to use it all, not just when we wanted. We had to climb 1200ft up the couloir, dump our gear and come back down to camp all in one afternoon. The climb started well with Steve leading again, me in the middle and Ant bringing up the rear. The sledge was coming up too but by now we had realised our mistake at bringing it along. It was going to be a nightmarish hindrance all the way to the summit and we had no need of extra baggage. We climbed alpine style as much as possible with Steve placing gear in the ice to protect a fall, me clipping past it as I followed and Ant picking it up from behind. This meant that we had to get together every few minutes to pass everything back to Steve but we could move quickly, rather than pitching rope all the way. The climb dragged on and on and before we knew it six hours had passed. Snow gave way to ice and then back to snow again. One moment I was teetering on the front points of my crampons, the next I was up to my knees in a snowdrift. Behind us the South Buttress rose out of the skyline dwarfing all around her as she meandered her way round to the summit. A little higher up the entire Alaska Range came into view with Mts. Foraker and Hunter peering out in the distance as tall sentinels overlooking this white land. The rocks, which marked the couloir edges started to narrow and we headed up to the right and met up on a small snow ledge. Steve laid a belay and we all clipped in.

Only a final traverse across some near vertical ice remained before we would be out of the couloir and onto a gentle snow slope. Steve nimbly crossed over and belayed himself to a long crack in the rock. I followed on, tiptoeing across the face not daring to look down. The ice was hard but rotten and I struggled to get a decent hold with either my crampons or axes. I teetered along step by step and breathed a sigh of relief when I clipped into the belay.

"Bloody hell Steve, that was hairy" I gasped. "Don't worry mate, you weren't going anywhere. I'd got you". He seemed so relaxed about it. If there were ever going to be times that were difficult, his steady head would keep things straight. Ant joined us and clipped himself in. "Right, then lads, up to the top then" said Steve.

He walked up towards a short ridge of compacted snow and belayed himself in. One by one we followed in procession until the ground levelled off and we could stand together. We had hoped to reach a campsite at about 13,000ft but we were 1000ft short and time was not on our side. A steady south-westerly wind had begun to blow bringing with it the ache of face stinging spindrift. It smacks into your cheeks like pebbles,

Ant climbing the Coulior

Seventeen days in

turning them cold and sore. "What do you reckon lads? "Steve asked. "We've got to get out of this, its bloody awful" replied Ant. "Too damn right" Steve replied. "I'll have a look up the ridge for somewhere to dig this lot in" I muffled from beneath layers of fleece.

I perilously approached a cornice trying to get a decent look up the ridge. The wind had slabbed the surface hard leaving ripples in the ice, like sand on a shoreline. The ground was stable, but I could see nothing uphill and downhill seemed a better place to dig in. I looked round a corner and with a sigh of relief found an ideal spot. "Down here lads, this'll do" I shouted and I jumped behind some rocks which looked straight down onto our camp, nearly 2000ft below. It looked a warm, inviting place in this now chilling situation. I could see the last few days' tracks weaving through the icefall. It all looked so easy from up here. The crevasses seemed small and insignificant but I knew their massive reality.

We all clambered onto the shelf and dropped our bags onto a deep drift. I grabbed the shovel from the back of my rucksack, smashed it into the snow and started digging like a madman. A yellow rope stared up at me from the hole. It was probably left after a rescue some time before but now it gave us something secure to tie to. We clipped the bags to it and hurriedly prepared to descend.

"We need to get down now lads, I'm bloody frozen" said Ant as he pulled on his down jacket. I threw the last shovel of snow onto the kit, pulled my snow goggles down over my eyes and headed for home. It was 9pm and the light was fading fast. We reversed the rope and Ant lead the downhill stretch for home. Grey shadows had engulfed the descent but the constant work of down climbing kept us all warm. We made new tracks in the couloir in an effort to preserve the earlier set for when we returned with the camp. It would be so easy to turn this slope from a steady climb into a torrid mess of fallen snow even with only the three of us. Ant seemed in one hell of a hurry to get home and I couldn't match his pace. I screamed "Ant, for gods sake slow down man, I can't keep up!" but the wind swallowed my words. All I could do was keep going as fast as my legs would take me and hope.

It took three hours of non-stop front pointing to get to the bottom of the couloir - it was nearly midnight and pitch dark.

We piled into the tents but made the mistake of not eating and drinking enough. The warm feel of my down sleeping bag was overpowering and drew me inside. The wind whistled around the camp all night but we were safe, warm and well dug in. The day had been hard and we all deserved a decent nights sleep. The cache was on the ridge and with it were my hopes for the summit and that's all that mattered.

After the exhausting grind of the last few days we deserved a day off. No one stirred until past ten when a chorus of muffled groans broke the silence. Still half asleep I pulled the tent zip open and looked outside. The sky was overcast and light cotton wool snow was falling gently to the ground. "Time to stay in bed I think Steve" I said. He agreed. Ant was still in his pit. I could hear a grinding snore echoing from inside his tent. For once, I had managed a good night's sleep and my eyelids were glued together.

I lit the stove for a morning brew and lay in bed staring at the icy ceiling in the tent. After an hour of daydreaming I eased out of bed to eat some breakfast. I sat up when a stab of pain ran down my back. I fumbled around for my first aid kit and threw some painkillers down to ease the dull ache. I really needed to sit up straight and stretch out my crumpled spine but mountain tents aren't built for such luxuries. Breakfast turned into brunch but after the last few days exertions our bodies had plenty of catching up to do. Today we had the time to stoke up the boilers at full throttle and recover.

All afternoon the sun struggled to break through the clouds. There was little movement on camp. Ant ventured out of his tent just the once all day. After a quick stretch and visit to the toilet he was back inside snuggling into his sleeping bag.

Whilst we lazed around, the American Team had disappeared up the couloir to drop off their supplies. They were back down for around 8pm and I was impressed with their speed. Geoff had 700ft of rope in his bag, which he intended to lay for the others to jumar up behind him.

I sat with the radio and bang on 8pm clicked the switch on. It cracked and spat for a few seconds until Annie's voice came hissing through. The signal was weak and fuzzy so I clamped my ear to the speaker and got the forecast - improving conditions for tomorrow but as I stared down the glacier, a thick cloud was beginning to settle.

I had set my alarm for 5am and with digital accuracy it attacked my eardrums with its electronic chorus. The air was bitter in the semi light of the tent but we had to make an early start. Steve reached out of the door and lit the stove. The roar hardly kept me awake but slowly I got the energy to assemble the brew kit and made the tea. The climbing was going to be hard and there was a camp to dig out and build high up the mountain. I was going to need all the energy I could get but I felt stiff and tired. We all lay silently eating breakfast before crawling out of the tents and breaking camp.

Walking the few hundred yards to the couloir, we passed the Americans camp. Geoff greeted us with a wave and a handshake. "We left the rope fixed last night. You guys can use it to jumar up if you want". It was a kind gesture. "You climbed fast yesterday Geoff, how did it go?" "Aahh, we didn't make it to the top. Our gear's about three quarters of the way up wedged onto a ledge". I was thankful for those few words. At least it proved we weren't too slow and they weren't superhuman. We bid him goodbye and waved to the others before we rounded the bend for the climb.

We clipped into Geoff's rope and worked slowly uphill until its last fixing into the ice. By the time I walked out onto the top my calves were aching from the constant front pointing into the icy sections. I had never felt ice so hard in my life.

All the time I was climbing, my fear of heights and of falling had never left me. You may find this a strange statement coming from someone in my position, but I have always been afraid of heights. It's never stopped me from doing things and I swallow my fears and suffer cold sweats but I manage as best as I can.

I was about to step onto the ridge when Steve dislodged a rock. It tumbled straight towards me but I had nowhere to go. Leaping out of the way was not an option. The cricket ball sized piece of granite bounced up and smashed into my right shin before continuing down the mountain. I hobbled over to a boulder, clipped in and sat down for a rest. My heart rate was high and I needed to calm down. I was lucky to escape with only a bruise and the slightest dribble of blood.

Over to the right, the Kahiltna Glacier was infested with rows of ant-sized climbers. Camp 1 was now a small village as commercial parties made their way to the Ranger Station in the Genet Basin. The climbers moved in slow procession in the deep snow and piled up into traffic jams. I was glad to be on a route that allowed the freedom I yearned for without the dawdling roped crowds.

After dropping into our cache we moved on, determined to make the 13,000ft high camp 4. Steve moved up along a divide between windswept snow and sun-bleached rock. To our left the drop was spectacular with rock outcrops bursting from the white sheets of glistening snow and ice dropping nearly 1000ft below.

After a couple of hour's slog, we reached what appeared

to be the campsite. It had again been a steep climb but good stable snow on the ridge had been easy to kick into and relatively safe. I stared downhill looking for a glimpse of the American Team but I couldn't see them. Had they gone down? Had something happened to them? We seemed much faster climbers than them today but surely not that much? In the distance, I spied a line of four ants up against a buttress of rock. They were still a long way down.

I collapsed into a deep drift and sank into its soft snow. It was so good to reach camp and rest. I stared into the beautiful distant plains far below but my dream world was broken with the immortal words "Lets get digging". Out of a small ledge of ice Steve and I began to dig out a tremendous bunker for the tents. Ant got tea on in-between helping us but a few cracks had begun to appear between us. I don't know whether he felt left out but words were exchanged quietly with Steve. What were they talking about? Was it about me? Had I done something wrong? The lateness of the day and the need to keep digging defused any confrontation and when we had finished building the camp we were too exhausted to argue.

A dull shout suddenly broke the evening air. "What was that?" I asked Steve. It came again "It's the yanks!" It was past 10pm and the Americans were still climbing. We thought they had camped further down as we hadn't heard anything and it was way past dark but they were still coming. Tony's silhouette appeared over the snows behind camp. He was hunched over and looked exhausted. "Anyone home?" he whimpered "Hi Tony. Where've you lot been?" came the reply. He began unfolding the story. They had climbed short fixed pitches, which as we knew took a great deal of time. One by One Geoff, Steve and Barbara came over and sat wearily down. "Fancy a brew?" asked Ant but he didn't need a reply. It was written all over their faces. He lit the stoves and boiled water whilst Steve and I grabbed shovels and began the job of digging out a terrace for their tents. A fever pitch of activity spread over the two camps. Torch beams pierced the darkness and powdery snow flew in clouds from the ground. We all took turns with the digging, which kept us warm. Ant pushed a cup of tea pushed into my hands and life felt even better.

A great sense of comradeship was appearing between us. This is what life is all about, not sitting to watch others struggle but to help wherever you can. Only then can man help himself with life and living, not ignorance and fighting. It took an hour to get camp built and then en masse we retreated inside our respective tents.

CHAPTER 3
THE WEST RIB

"Nige, it's eight o'clock, we'd better get moving!" Steve looked at his watch to find we had slept through the alarm an hour ago. "Must have been all that work yesterday" I groaned and rolled over in my bag. He was soon lighting the stove and getting breakfast on. We had become good friends on the trip although we had only met a few months before. He was slim, very fit and loved his climbing. As for Ant, I had known him for a few years but we only met occasionally due to work pressures and our own life objectives. We had met through Raleigh International. He had been to Guyana and I to Chile. We saw each other at the parties and reunions which Raleigh seems to create. He was a happy go lucky bloke who worked and played hard, very hard.

We descended yesterday's footprints to our cache. We arrived at our kit within a couple of hours and split up the weight before moving back towards camp. I tried to lift my rucksack but I could hardly get it off the ground. It clanged onto the floor and the smell of fuel began to rise from inside. I looked around but as far as I could tell the cans were intact, at least for now. Although the packs were lightening, altitude was having its say. Sleeping high up was helping with the acclimatisation but still my lungs were struggling with the thinning air and terrific weights. We walked into camp after a couple of hours. Plastic bags were strewn everywhere containing everything from tea and coffee to pasta, rice, potato powder, biscuits, jerky and of course, Ant's cooking spices. We sat and drank a well-earned brew before deciding what to do next. Should we push on further with the cache or rest for the afternoon? There was hardly anything to say. We all looked at each other and without a single word we began to pack. A few minutes later we were roped up and ready to go.

Steve had done all the hard work lately, so I lead off. The first ice dome went slowly. To our right, the ice was rock hard and terribly exposed. I tiptoed across the edge and buried a snow stake into the ground. Wisps of cloud had begun to form in the distance but they seemed miles away. Nevertheless a front was coming in and we had to be quick. I climbed onto a sharp ridge leading up to some easier ground. From what I could see the snow levelled out before rising again towards an outcrop of rocks in the distance. The cloud was thickening, and a steady breeze had begun to blow. I kept going onto the plateau, hoping to make the rocks before the weather forced us down. The visibility was failing and we all huddled together and took a look at the map. We were at about 14,000ft, not far below the Bergschrund Camp, but we would not make it there today. "This will do lads. Let's just bury the kit and get down," said Ant. The conditions were deteriorating rapidly, but we had done well and a warm camp was waiting for us below. We piled everything into a hole and covered it with snow. Ant pushed a wand in the snow to mark the cache and we set off down to camp. A cold chill rattled my bones and I was glad to be heading for the tents. We reached camp at 8.30pm, tired and bedraggled, but happy. My shoulders cried with freedom as I eased the rucksack straps off them and put the bag down. I was sore and sweaty, but without a care.

I dozed through the early morning alarm again - Steve did not. His rummaging around soon got me out of my warm bed. It was −10C but the day looked clear and calm. We had been so lucky with the weather, so far anyway. I dragged myself outside and stood staring outward to the limitless plains in the distance. This really was frontier country. To think, only a century ago prospectors came this way to find their fortunes in gold. We now came to find our souls and climb.

Muffled voices sounded from inside the tents above us. Tony opened his door and looked outside. His slick Californian voice broke the bitter air "Hey guys, howya doin'?" "We're fine mate" replied Steve. "How are you?" "Great! You off up the mountain again today?" "Yes!"

The day was beautifully clear and began to warm up very quickly. The cold I brought with me had now disappeared due to a constant bombardment of tablets. Ant had kept a watchful eye over me, reminding my conscience of the times I forgot my medication and it had worked. I led again and strode confidently onward over the dome and back onto the plateau. Yesterday's tracks were clearly defined up the slope and in the distance I could see the little wand marking our cache. We were there in no time. A hot soup warmed my insides and stung my cracked lips but it was still lovely. There we were, basking out in the sun with not a care in the world. Above us, shadowed by a large Bergschrund was tonight's camp. It took another three hours of slog uphill before we at last threw down our bags.

Although the mass of ice above us was cold, it did give good weather protection. After chipping a base away for the tents we sat admiring the view. I stood up. "Grab your axe's Steve!" I stood against the Bergschrund and kicked my crampons deeply into the ice face, then smashed in both axes above my head. "Get a photo quick!" Steve snapped away and I returned the favour. The backdrop was incredible and below us looked into a tremendous ice cave. A lonely voice then sounded from behind the ice. "Teas up!" Ant had sat patiently and done all the cooking and he was clearly unhappy. The tension lasted only a few moments before we were engaged in stuffing the hot food into our mouths. Something had been wrestling in my mind for the last few days about how we were getting on together but I couldn't place it. Something seemed wrong but nothing had been said. Something would have to give sometime and that time didn't feel far away.

Annie's forecast for the next few days was for good, clear conditions with light winds. I just hoped we would be allowed an attempt at the summit before any fronts came in and broke the peace above our heads.

Jumaring on the West Rib – Photo Antony Hollinshead

Summit Day on the Orient Express

My bleary eyes stared mistily into my watch. It was 6.45am. A milky light was staring at me from the inner of the tent and I couldn't remember when it had last been this light this early in a morning. For once, we had camped in a position to catch the morning sun and it was lovely to get up into a warm tent. The rising odour from our sleeping bags grasped my lungs at the first breath and I coughed loudly. Usually it would have brought the house down as the icicles would shower me but in the warm air, there was no ice. Water replaced it and began running down the inner and dripping down my back. Steve opened the tent door and threw the sleeping bags into the sun to dry. Ant had got the breakfast on still lying in his steaming pit. Outside, the day looked marvellous with more miles of mountains, blue skies and little cloud.

The uphill slog of yesterday became a jog down the mountain to pick up our supplies. I laughed inside at being able to make good progress for once, but the problem was that we were going downhill, not up! We raced to the cache, pulled the wand from out of the snow and frantically dug out the shallow bags and fuel cans. I was full of energy and let my mind race away, ignoring the situation around me.

Ant had sat down, pondered for a moment and stared up into the sky. He had a dejected look all over his face. "Lads, we need to talk". Those few words shattered my apparent happiness. "What's up Ant?" Steve asked. "I'm not happy with how everything's going". "Go on". "Well, it's the way you two are working, how I'm always doing the cooking, I feel left out, as if I'm not here." The conversation clearly highlighted the tensions which I had noticed over the last few days but were too scared to confront.

Ant was very unhappy at the way Steve and I were running camp, sticking together and doing the route planning and to be honest they were all valid points, although I felt that he always wanted to be at the back of the rope and you can't lead from there. He was slow at getting up in a morning and dawdled sometimes. I know we all took photographs which held us up from time to time, but Ant took an age, his camera action was slow and we would get cold standing about. He would always be shouting, "Hold on lads, just another shot before we go" as he fumbled with his lenses. He felt left out in the group and even talked of going on alone but in my mind that was not an alternative. This was a team effort and nothing else.

Ant was right about the cooking and we decided to take turns at playing mother. He did complain about the amount of height we were gaining and camps we were choosing but I didn't agree. He was concerned we were going too high too fast and I did not. All of us had done well in the circumstances and showed no signs of severe altitude sickness so far. We were short of breath but up here that is a part of life and we only had three and a half weeks to climb the lot and get home. There was plenty of time in my mind provided the weather didn't stop us. As for the camps, I thought that we had done very well with what was on offer. The small numbers of climbers on the route had allowed excellent sites. If there had been big groups then everyday would have been a race for the best camping spot. I have been in this predicament before and all it does is breed altitude sickness, arguments and danger. We talked for around half an hour and every word was said calmly and discussed thoroughly, before hands were duly shaken and points taken. This truly was democracy in action and I hoped it would save any bitterness as we climbed further up the mountain which was a better situation than arguing at 20,000ft!

Steve stepped into a small crevasse and fell backwards down the slope. "I'm falling!" he screamed as he rolled over and over into ever deepening snow. Well, what else could he say? I fell to my knees to bury my axe shafts and stop him but my feet slipped from under me and I ended up sliding down the slope myself. Ant stood above us and stared down in disbelief at the tangled mass of legs, ropes and rucksacks below him. Both Steve and I had sunk into deep snowdrifts and stopped. Ant had never even moved. We were plastered in white from head to foot but uninjured. I stood up and beat the powder from my body. It had found every gap in my clothing and filled both my neck and cuffs. I shook both arms and released cascades of white into the air before rubbing my back and dumping the damp snow from my skin. It sent a shiver down my spine not only physically but also mentally as we picked ourselves up and regained our slightly dented pride.

The climb started well enough, but again we hit hard ice. No matter how much we slammed our axes into its glassy face, they bounced off like rubber. Our cramponed feet scraped and slipped at every step but Steve led a daring 50ft section to the safety of the ridge and wedged himself into the rocks. He screamed down that he was safe and I was to follow him up. He took the slack on the rope and I began my climb towards him. I made a terrible mess of it. No matter how hard I tried I couldn't stand on my front points hard enough whilst balancing the gigantic rucksack on my back. I wouldn't say I climbed the section at all. It was more like a shuffle and a shimmy between rocks and rope, and anything else I could get a grip on. Eventually, Steve held out an arm, grabbed my bag and hauled me up to safety. I rolled onto my back and perched myself between two boulders. Sweat was running down my face and my nerves weak. 'What am I doing here?' I thought to myself. Without Steve's help, I could never have managed the last few feet at all and I felt such a fool between the two much better climbers. If anything went wrong up here I would probably be the reason for it and for that I felt ashamed.

Time was running short and dusk was falling fast. I secured the bags to a rock and abseiled off the rib. The temperature was plummeting and we had been stood still far too long. We had to pendulum repeatedly left and right on the rope to miss kicking loose rocks onto the camp below. Ant rushed down with another of his breakneck descents dragging Steve and I down behind him. I was almost pulled over again and again but Ant had smelled the tents and there was no stopping him. We jumped over the last crevasse and rounded the corner into camp. By now, the air was biting into my lungs but the homely roar of the stoves and a hot drink soon lifted my spirits.

Once again we slept through the numerous watch alarms. "Time to get up lads!" Ant shouted. It was 8am. In a sudden frenzy, the camp became alive. Gear was packed, breakfast cooked and camp was struck. Since our disagreements of yesterday we suddenly worked better and much faster. "At least something was going right," I thought to myself. "I've still got to get onto that bloody ridge though and keep going up".

We had to get right up the rib today and make for the 16,000ft camp. That's nearly 2000ft of climbing but there was little alternative. No other campsites existed and we had to be the first to claim the spot. All the guides said that it would be as high as we could go unless we risked a very exposed camp. Positions on the ridge are rare enough but at least they can offer some shelter when you are on the leeward side of them. Above the ridge there was nothing but exposed ice and snow and stories of tents being blown apart were common.

Walking out from camp, I spotted the American Team moving slowly up the dome a thousand or so feet below us. They were heading for our camp, another one we had made ready for them. I felt as if they were letting us do all the hard work and then just following on behind. We had navigated the icefall and crevasse fields, laid a track up the gulley and dug nearly all the camps out. There was some resentment in my thoughts but we had become great friends and we would beat them to the summit. I didn't know if that mattered now.

Most of my racing instincts seemed to have faded away and the lads didn't talk about it either. Perhaps the mountain was calming me down as reality eased into my thoughts.

It didn't take long to reach yesterday's ice climb to the ridge. Steve had left a rope fixed last night which made it only a short jumar to our cache. I was glad of being able to pull myself up but the bags weighed heavy today and the 150ft climb hurt my already tiring muscles. Altitude not only makes the job harder but it slows down your recovery too. The body cries out for oxygen to replenish the muscles lost energy but at this height the levels are low and so recovery is slow. My arms screamed for more energy at every push of the jumar but there was little to spare. You just have to plod on, and on, and on. My mind suddenly went out of control with a surge of adrenaline and inside I jumped. "I will beat this bloody hill, just you watch me!" It said, and like some kind of crazed madman I shot up the rope and sat straddling the cache. "All yours Ant!" I screamed. The few seconds' exertion then caught up with me and pounded into my already aching head. "Why did I do that?" I calmly thought. It's a bit like having one of those hideous red wine headaches when moving your head hurts like hell. Unfortunately, I had no wine to blame my agony on. The lads joined me and we sat eating a little dinner until Steve looked down at his watch, "Bloody hell! Come on lads, it's four o'clock". Time had flown by and we were still a long way from camp.

Ant and I sat for ages belaying an invisible Steve. He had disappeared around some rocks and was leading his way up the ridge. We shouted again and again but the growing wind swept our voices away into the clouds. I shuffled along the thin rocky edge daring for a look round the corner at where he was but I couldn't see a thing. Again I shouted and above me a little head appeared in the distance. "Give us a minute Nige, I'm just setting up". It was a relief to see Steve safe but the pace was painfully slow. Ant and I were getting cold on the exposed rock face and there seemed only deteriorating weather ahead. "Alright, up you come lads," boomed Steve and I clipped my jumar onto the rope once more.

After another arm wrenching session I was perched on a towering rock with only a sling thrown over a dangerous looking face for protection. I lay there rigid, slowly being covered in snow until I almost disappeared in the whiteness. Bad weather was closing in and the snow and steady breeze made me shiver. The cloud made route finding almost impossible, as we couldn't see much more than 100ft. Ant joined me on the rock and once again Steve shot up the route. A procession of snow ridges and easy rock led upward to a small plateau - it was beautiful and a blessed relief. The cloud had obscured the vertical exposure making my life considerably easier. We dusted snow off each other regularly and took scores of pictures. It was past nine in the evening but there was still enough light to see a few hundred feet. I pulled my glasses away from my squinting eyes and parked them across my hat brim to see the greying snow. The campsite was still a couple of hours away and I was getting cold. Above us, a lonely star rose from the west, nature's twilight messenger announcing that the night was coming.

The climbing guides had given us a shaky description of this campsite and we had one hell of a job trying to find it. We eventually dropped our bags under a small outcrop of rocks before searching up the icy ridge for the unknown hovel. There was nothing to hand. Back in Talkeetna the Rangers had described to us a very dodgy place to sleep - The "Sucker Camp". That was visible up ahead but there was no way on earth we were camping there in this wind. It was at 16,500ft and completely exposed. Any sharp breeze would rip our tents clean off the ice and down the mountain with us in them. It was not a place for the faint hearted, only the daring and the stupid. With our tails between our legs, we retreated back to the bags and decided to camp under the rocks.

With an explosion of energy, I smashed my snow shovel into the drifts and began digging. It was early morning and we had to work fast. Steve and I had the largest tent so we camped right under the outcrop - Ant being on his own camped at the side. It was as icy as hell and the axes were needed to finish the site. It was 3.30am when we finally got inside the tents. I lay down onto my sleeping bag and slowly pulled off my boots. Both of my feet were completely numb. My hands weren't far behind them and I zipped myself into my bag and wriggled around hoping the circulation would return.

My eyes didn't crack open until midday but I had managed little sleep - the altitude was starting to take its effect. I opened the tent door and shook off the fresh snow. Camp had been dusted with an inch of powder which was just enough to cover last night's tracks. The crystals were clean and bright and had buried the gear we had wedged between the rocks. Here we sat in the heavens with the clouds below us and only a few peaks islanded above the white fluffy sea. A gentle breeze stirred the powder into minute whirlwinds which ran silently along the ledge. I lay on my bag, stripped down to my shorts and enjoyed the warmth of the tent. My feet had recovered from last night's escapade and my hands, though hard and chapped were fine. The stoves were on and a piping cup of tea soon warmed through my body. Inside I felt tired but relaxed. With a loud rustle of frozen Pertex Ant popped his head out from his tent and shouted "Hello chaps, how's it going"? "Not bad Ant" replied Steve. "Good night's kip?" "Not bad. Bit cold!" Not much else happened all morning. We just lay in and dozed.

Ant joined us around 4pm and squeezed himself into our already bursting tent. Food, food and more food was the order of the day with plenty of drinks to combat the dehydration. We needed to stock up as best we could for the summit push, should it come. For the first time in days, we cracked jokes together and laughed. We were all seasoned travellers and the usual expedition stories begun to appear. Everything from swimming with piranhas, catching malaria, eating rancid rations and describing gory wounds seemed to bring a laugh. This was the first time on the entire trip that we had been together in one tent. The stoves roared all evening as we talked but outside the wind had begun to pick up and spindrift flew around the camp.

The forecast at 8pm brought "clear skies up to 20,000ft but wind speed increasing up to 50mph at the summit. "Keep it together up there!" said Annie. The prospect of sleeping this high in that wind made me shudder. We made sure the tents were well pegged down for the night and fought around in the darkness with our head torches blazing through the dark skies. I lay in my bag watching the tent poles contort backwards and forwards all evening. The walls baffled and banged under the wind's power and I struggled to shut out the deafening racket from my mind. "I don't like this Steve," I said. "I'm worried". "It's alright Nige, we're well battened down, don't worry mate. We'll be fine" he replied confidently but all night I lay rigid with fear.

Next morning it was still gusty but bright sunlight flooded the mountainsides. We descended to the last of our supplies and fully established the camp at 16,300ft. The possibility of a quick summit dash had been halted and we could afford a few days grace to wait for the weather to clear.

On the descent we met the Americans. Steve and Barbara decided to drop down to the Ranger Camp in the Genet Basin and complete the climb via the Washburn Route whilst Geoff and Tony would be following us straight up the Rib. They were still a day behind so this meeting was to be our farewell - for a while anyway. "See you in Talkeetna for a beer," Geoff laughed. We had shaken hands and said our goodbyes before abseiling over the edge to the ridges below. We had one disaster that afternoon – Steve lost a glove. I had given him my spare mitts to get us home but his hand had become dangerously cold in seconds and taught us a quick lesson in wind-chill.

The next morning Ant gave a shout from his tent. A rock had rolled down the ice in the darkness and struck his tent, breaking a pole and tearing the fabric. He had slept the rest of the night with his helmet on. The repair kit was hardly sufficient to make a decent job but with a little brute force, some imagination and an ice screw I managed to force in a repair sleeve. "I don't know how long it'll last Ant but it's as good as it will get up here" I said and handed him his bent aluminium pole.

We huddled together realising a decision had to be made but no one would break the silence. The big question was were we on for tomorrow or not? Anxiously we waited for the 8pm forecast. "How's about going up with Tony and Geoff? A sort of Anglo American attempt?" I suggested. Steve and Ant agreed. We knew Geoff was tremendously experienced and between the five of us we had a better chance of getting onto the summit. The idea of a race was now gone. It had become too serious to joke about. Time was getting short for us. It was Tuesday now, and we flew home to England next Wednesday.

I turned on the radio just before 8pm. "Tomorrow on the mountain there will be winds of 20-30mph with possible light snow showers". We decided to go for it. Steve and Ant were already dressed up to go and find the Americans. I had both stoves working overtime to boil up water for each of us tomorrow. The lads returned after an hour or so without finding anyone. "Perhaps they've camped at 17,000ft?" I suggested. "There are tracks going up that way," replied Ant "but we'll be out there all night looking if they are".

We all looked at each other with excited gazes. "That's it then. We need to be up at five to stand any chance," said

Steve. A fever of activity graced the tent for the next hour as the summit day gear was packed. I dived into my bag as soon as I could and tried to sleep. My eyes began to close as the sun fell and the lonely stars filled the night sky.

CHAPTER 4
TOGETHER ONE LAST TIME

I awoke and felt my fingers and toes tingle. Everything looked the right colour but they felt cool to touch. It was 5am and I felt sure that once we were moving everything would be fine. Outside, the sky was a dull red with few clouds and little wind. Everything looked perfect but the day didn't start well. One stove failed to light - probably blocked jets, yet we had only cleaned them a few days before. Breakfast was delayed by a good hour but this was not the day we wanted delays. We had to be up and out. The air was blisteringly cold and forcing our warm bodies out of our comfortable sleeping bags was hard work. By the time we were ready to go, it had turned half past eight. I stood outside and looked over the tents towards the summit. It looked daunting, massive and a bit scary but I felt sure that by the end of the day we would stand on top of the mountain. This was going to be the hardest days climbing of my life.

We passed the Sucker Camp with ease and moved towards the main ascent of the day, the dreaded Orient Express, so named due to the number of Orientals who have died on it. Its 6000ft of curving ice had spat many a victim into the Genet Basin, ricocheting them down the rocks like a pinball. For a change Ant led and rather than risk a direct assault he moved to the right and climbed between the rocks and boulder fields for protection. The going was hard, as high winds had blasted the fresh snow away, leaving old hard ice on the surface. My bones soon began to shake in the extreme cold but before I could say anything Steve screamed "Come on Ant, I'm freezing!" I could see that Ant was frustrated. His crampons were scratching on the ice and his axes were doing little better. He shouted at himself and the ice but he was getting nowhere. Suddenly Steve shot past me and began climbing. This left me belaying both of them from a very dodgy position. Cold and impatience had taken their toll on Steve and he was off. Not knowing quite what to do, I moved up behind the pair of them to regain some balance between us all. The pace now hotted up and within no time, we had found the 17,300ft camp.

Shreds of tent littered the icy floor. Aluminium poles stood like lonely gravestones marking the spot of some past disaster. Strangely out of place was a well-staked pile of equipment in the centre of this devastation. A pair of Italian climbers had been hot on our trail a day or two back - perhaps it was theirs? I took over the lead and smashed my crampons deep into the snow. A thin crust of windslab covered the slope but it was easy to kick out deep steps with my size eleven feet. I made straight for a patch of rock 100yds above. They gave me some welcome shelter and a good point to belay. I pounded a piton into a crack and attached a karibiner. There is a wonderful sense of security when you hear the click of the screw gate close over the rope. It's like the blanket you had as a child coming to life again.

Light snow was beginning to fall but I felt good inside. It was as if a magical rush of energy had filled my body. The altitude was having little effect on me and I felt like a child wanting to run all day and night. I set off again with a mad rush and made the last set of rocks before we broke onto the summit plateau. My fingers were suffering from cold and I fumbled with the rope as I clipped into the snow stake. I took off my outer glove, pushed it under my armpit and protected only by my thin liners, my freezing fingers slammed the rope home. The relief was instant but it was smashed as I watched my glove sail down the slope into oblivion. "Bloody hell!" I thought. "You prat Nigel, what are you going to do now?" I screamed and shook in anger but remembered that I had my big mittens in my rucksack. Thank God I had, otherwise my fingers wouldn't have lasted long in the cold air. The temperature was well below zero and falling.

I looked down the slope to see two distant figures climbing towards Ant and Steve. There seemed to be some talking going on between them and I hoped that it was Geoff and Tony coming to join us but they soon left and went back down the mountain. When the lads joined me I found out they were a couple of American climbers who had come from the camp in the Genet basin and were acclimatising.

We had reached an important decision point. Above us stood three snow plastered gullies. We chose the middle one keeping to its left side, but by now I was worn out. Over 2000ft of leading had taken its toll on my body and I was flagging. I pulled on my down jacket and took a rest. Steve took over and within a few minutes he was forcing through the final section of rocks to the top. It was late in the day and a steady wind was picking up but the light was still good and together we felt strong. It was less than a mile's walk to the summit. We had to make it – it seemed so close.

I climbed the gully and clambered over the rocks onto the plateau. The wind instantly hit me and drove a biting cold through my gear. Spindrift tore across the plateau and rattled against my goggles. Only two thirds of a mile to go. I struggled with the map but managed to take a compass bearing. I pointed the needle towards the summit. There was nothing in sight – swirling cloud had taken the visibility down to only a few hundred yards.

"Let's dump all the spare kit and go for it" Steve shouted, "Right, it shouldn't take long" I replied. A pile of axes and ropes were smashed into the ice as a marker for our return journey home in a few hours time. Roped together we walked across the plateau towards our goal. We were face on to the weather and my hood broke loose in the wind. I struggled to secure it and Ant had to clip it down with a karabiner. The situation was worsening. Poor visibility, biting cold and the uneven ice made progress painfully slow. We would take a few steps forward before a gust would blow us back like paper bags. Ant was planting wands behind us to help find the way home and suddenly cried "Nige, the summits over to the left!" "Where?" I screamed - the cloud had smothered it almost instantly. "It's not far away". "We'll keep going then, it won't be long now". The winds power began to increase and it became apparent that Ant was not happy. We reached a small crest in the ice. "Let's take the photos here and get down. No one will know," cried Ant. "We've come all this way Ant, were not stopping now!" replied Steve and I was right behind him. This had been a long hard climb and the last few hundred yards were not going to defeat us.

My left eye was beginning to weep heavily. The cold was biting through my goggles and layers of insulation and freezing my cheek. I couldn't see much anyway, but this made things worse. "Nige, you've got to keep your face covered". Ant was staring at my now frozen nose and cheek. A thin layer of ice had moulded round my face and froze the tissue solid. I tried to pull my balaclava up but it fell down repeatedly. Eventually with Ant's help, I sealed the gap and we pushed on.

The ground before us began to rise. We were nearly there - only a few yards to go. The clouds cleared and the top of the Cassin Ridge appeared. We were on the wrong side of the summit! The wind had pushed us to the right and off course. I was chilled almost to the bone but except for my face, I was ok as long as we kept moving. Steve however began to look drained. Hypothermia was beginning to set in. He complained of the cold and began to lose coordination. We had to get out of the wind. Its tremendous force was sapping the heat from our bodies every second. It was late in the day and the sun was falling. I realised that we were in a very serious situation. We needed to get out of the blasting gusts and shelter Steve but the plateau offered no shelter and we looked around madly for somewhere to hide.

At the base of the summit slope, Ant found a small crevasse lying horizontally in the ice. It looked hopeful. With furious swings of our axes, we opened up the thin gap chip by chip, enough to slide ourselves inside. We all knew that the situation was bad. If only we could warm up a little we would be fine and I prayed the wind would stop, at least for a while. Last night's forecast had said nothing about this weather but I knew that summit storms could last for days. If this was one of them we truly were in the mire. We took off our rucksacks and slid down into the crevasse.

Steve was shivering very slowly. His body was beginning to give in and go into collapse. Ant looked straight into my eyes "Nige, we've got to hug round Steve and try to warm him up!" We wrapped our arms around his freezing body and held on for dear life. Outside the wind howled across the mountain, but it all seemed to disappear when Steve began to talk. He ranted on about how we were saving him, his home life, family, friends and whatever entered his wandering mind. It was horrible to hear but at least he was alive. Time passed as if in a dream and after a while I drifted off into an uncomfortable sleep. I wanted so much to stay awake but my body was spent and could do no more. How long I was out I don't know but I woke and peered over the icy ledge to stare across the plateau outside. In the distance the sun had set over the mountains. A purple haze hugged the horizon and the magenta clouds slowly faded into semi darkness. I slid back down to Steve and Ant and closed my eyes again.

CHAPTER 5
AFTER THE SUNSET

I don't remember when I woke up. Time had become an irrelevance. Outside, the wind was still tearing across the plateau and a dim light flooded across the ice. I struggled up to peer over the crevasse edge and saw the sun slowly rising and the sky lighting up. I couldn't feel my feet and both my hands were like ice. What was happening to me? I tried to put the thought of frostbite to the back of my mind but it just kept coming back as I sat there and shivered. Ant and Steve looked no better. They were still huddled together and white over with frost. Ant looked over at me and said. "Nige, try the radio and contact base camp". Why no one had thought of this before I'll never know. Perhaps the cold really was getting to our minds. I fumbled in my bag and pulled out the radio. The batteries were hidden in my pockets to keep them warm and my fingers stung as I tried to open the battery compartment and clip them in one by one. I closed the compartment and turned on the switch. The set crackled into life.

I started to call "Hello Kahiltna Base, Hello Kahiltna Base, this is DENSAN, DENSAN, do you read, over". Nothing came back. I tried again. Still nothing. I kept going until I suddenly realised a fatal mistake in the make up of the unit - it was a CB radio. It needed direct line of sight to be heard. Lying down in the crevasse was hopeless. I had to get outside in the open and call again. I shuffled out a little into the wind. I thought the shelter of the snow hole was cold but outside was dreadful. The wind bit through my clothes in seconds. I called again, still nothing. "Keep trying Nige!" shouted Ant. I fought the cold with what little energy I had left and kept calling.

Suddenly a muffled voice came through. "This is Kahiltna Base. I cannot understand you. Say again, over". At last – contact. To hear that distant voice gave us hope, hope a long way away, but at least hope. I started again -. "Hello Kahiltna Base, this is DENSAN, DENSAN, over". It was no use. Through the static and hissing we could hear them but they could not hear us. Base Camp had a twenty-foot tall Ariel and pile of warm batteries. They could burst through the storm easily, but the hand held unit that I used was frozen solid and 20,000ft up the mountain. "This is Kahiltna Base. Use your transmit button to answer our calls. One click for yes, two clicks for no. Over". "Roger that". The questions came thick and fast. They had a full inventory of who was on the mountain and they worked through the expedition names systematically. Where we one team, then another? It seemed an endless job and I was getting dangerously cold out in the open but I had to sit it out. I heard a crackled DENSAN. I clicked the ptt switch with relief. At least now they knew who we were, our route, what gear we had and roughly where we were. "Is anybody injured?" One click. "Can they walk?" Two clicks. Are you near the summit? One click. Do you require a rescue?" One click. The cold was becoming unbearable but I had to stay in touch. "There are no rescue teams available to get to you for two or three days. We'll send up a plane to spot for you at eight am. Turn your radio off to save the batteries until you here hear the plane". The radio went silent. I slid down the ice and back into the relative warmth of the crevasse.

Inside, little had changed. Steve and Ant were still huddled in the corner. "How's Steve?" I asked. "He's still with us," replied Ant. "They're putting up a plane at 8am to find us but we can't expect any help for two or three days. We can't stay up here waiting for them to come, we'll be frozen solid". Ant agreed. There would only be three blocks of ice for the rescuers to find – all of them dead and gone.

I then witnessed the most incredible thing I have ever seen in the mountains - Steve began to come around. "How are you doing mate?" asked Ant. "I've felt better Ant, I'm bloody freezing". No one could disagree about that, we were almost frozen through but all we could do was wait for the plane to come. I guessed it was four or five o'clock but I didn't risk stripping the layers from my hands and wrist to look. The radio batteries were frozen solid and almost flat. I pushed it deep into a pocket and prayed that with a little warmth inside it, the set would work again.

Nearer to 8am I pulled the radio from my coat and placed it against the crevasse entrance ready for the planes flight. Within a second, it had fallen over the edge and down the slope into the distance. In pulling myself up, out of the crevasse I had clipped it with my elbow. My eyes filled with horror and I screamed in fury. After a few seconds it stopped and sat as a tiny black dot on the ice. "What's wrong Nige?" Shivered Ant. I was filled with embarrassment. "The radio's gone" I replied. I couldn't believe I had wasted our only means of communication with the outside world. If we never got out it of this alive, it would be my fault. I sat back in the hole and said nothing. The silence was unbearable. Steve said, "Look lads. There's no way they're going to come up here and get us. Let's see if we can get down on our own. It's the only way". Outside the wind had dropped a little and it was certainly light. Could this be our only means of survival?

Outside it was cloudy and cold but otherwise bearable. I looked down at the Radio and decided to fetch it in the vain hope it still worked. I slowly stood up and tried to walk but my feet wouldn't move - they were frozen through to the bone. My body was already lurching forward and I fell heavily onto the ice. I bounced along screaming in fear with ice pouring into my face stinging, my nose and cheeks. My goggles filled with snow and I was blind. Suddenly, I stopped. No rope had caught me but the ripples in the ice had slowed me down enough. I cleared my goggles and saw the radio sitting beside me. I felt I deserved at least a little luck. I picked it up and turned it on. It looked in one piece but was now silent. Something inside was broken and it was useless. Another pang of guilt ran through my bones. I had been an idiot to lose such a valuable piece of equipment. There was nothing I could do but hobble up the slope and rejoin the lads. How would I tell them about the radio?

I stumbled towards the crevasse and heard the faint noise of a propeller. I thought at first it was some kind of joke my mind way playing but it got louder and louder. A plane was circling around the mountain. They had come! Steve and Ant came outside but broken cloud was lying above the mountain and no matter how much we shouted or waved, they didn't see us. It was a devastating moment. So close to contact, yet with no means to talk. The radio could have saved us all there and then.

We put on our climbing gear and set off for camp. The journey back to the Orient Express should have been relatively easy and we could down climb to our tents and warm up properly there. The sun was up and although breezy it was nothing compared to last nights tornado. The wands were easy to see but my feet had been devastated by frostbite. Standing on them was painful – walking was proving unbearable. Ant put me on a short rope and led me out towards home. My left cheek had become more inflamed and I could see little if anything at all from my eye. I stumbled on every piece of ice imaginable and I fell down every few yards. I kept getting up and continued walking, but the pace was painfully slow. I clenched my teeth in the hope of deflecting the pain of my feet away but it did little. Every time I fell, I cursed even more and I felt a hindrance to both Steve and Ant. Years ago filmmakers would have loved a scene such as this. There would have been a "leave me chaps and save yourselves" scene. But this was not 1930 and I was not Errol Flynn. Every time I fell, Ant patiently helped me up and we kept going but we were all getting colder. I was half blinded, frost-bitten and losing my mind.

We found the gear we had left at the top the Orient Express. At least we were on the right route home but now we had to take a decision. "We'll never get Nige down the express safely" Ant said to Steve. Of course he was right. Steve pondered. "Well, we'll have to go for the Washburn route and find a high camp to get a radio message through". For days we had seen climbers ascending high onto the mountain above the Genet Basin. We just had to hope someone was there. For all we knew all hell could be breaking loose below us, due to our mayday messages.

Slowly we moved on but it was hopeless. I was in no state to walk. The landscape began to change and rocks began to appear, jutting from the ice. It was only a matter of time before we had to think of something else. I was a wreck. Physically and mentally drained, I sat down on a rock. My body was almost entirely frozen and battered to pieces from falling over. I didn't feel defeated, just very pissed off and a failure. A failure to myself but more importantly a failure to both Steve and Ant. Hypothermia was slowing my mind's reflexes and I struggled to hear them talking. I knew a conversation was going on but about what I had no idea. Before I realised it Steve walked away from us and in minutes was gone. It was like watching a ghost disappear into the mist but I couldn't understand why. "Where was he going?" I thought to myself. I was unable to face the reality until it struck hard home. He was going to descend alone for help. Ant was staying with me. It must have been near midday as the sun was high but I was still bitterly cold. Ant wedged the pair of us between two large rocks for shelter and there we waited – it was all we could do.

I had to drink something. It had been at least 18 hours since any liquid had passed my lips and I was parched. I drew my bottle from its thermal liner and forced the stopper open with an ice axe. Inside it was frozen solid. Ant was in the same dilemma. We pushed our bottles under our layers of fleece and down in an attempt to thaw something but we were cooling ourselves in the process. This was a no win situation. Without liquid, frostbite would be worse as it dwells on dehydration but by having the bottles inside our clothes we were colder. I rooted further into my bag for some food. All I found was one sweet; the rest had taken off in last night's blizzard. I sucked slowly hoping it would last longer. Its sugars rolled around my mouth in an almost blissful state.

Slowly the wind changed direction and we were exposed to its icy grasp once more. We moved around the rocks and found some shelter a few feet away. Ant and I huddled together like an old couple on a park bench. Long periods of silence were occasionally broken by questions of what if...? Should we...? Will they...?

A steady drone began to fill the air. It got louder and louder. It was a helicopter! Steve must have got through to someone and called for a rescue! It must have been a superhuman effort by him but he must have done it. Below us a thin layer of cloud covered the Genet Basin and the helicopter from our sight. Ant had been trying to fix the radio and began to call out but there was no reply. The rotors sounded louder and louder, but faded away taking our hopes with them. For the next few hours, this game of cat and mouse continually raised our hopes and then shattered them. All they had to do was rise a few hundred feet through the cloud and they would see us but neither of our eyes met and we were left silent and alone again.

The white daylight began to fade into crimson sunset. I didn't know if I would be able to stand another night exposed to the elements and still survive. What would I be like in the morning? I thought. I pulled my rucksack over my legs and prepared myself as best as I could for the coming freeze. I huddled up to Ant and prayed for salvation. For some unknown reason, the thought of death never entered my mind as my thoughts had slowed almost to a halt. Something was working though as I gained the insane desire to see one of my hands. I just had to look at what it was like. I tentatively drew the liner glove off my right hand to be confronted with a contortion of ivory white fingers that I could not move. My little finger seemed in an impossible position, frozen through to the bone. My eyes filled and heart fell. Frostbite had turned into a morbid reality.

Struggling to replace my gloves, I heard another distant drone. "Here we go a bloody 'gain" I thought, but rising from the clouds came the silhouette of a helicopter. It headed straight for us. Below it was a bag suspended by a rope. It came in close and blasted snow high into the air before dropping a bag. Within seconds it was gone and silence once again prevailed. I was stunned by how quick it had happened but overjoyed that we had been found. Steve had got a message through.

No-matter how frostbitten I was, I ran for the bag and dragged it over to Ant. We fumbled with the catches, before opening it. Inside was a steel Thermos flask. We ripped off the lid and threw back the hot juice. I burned my lips and scorched my throat but I didn't care. The feeling of warmth inside me was incredible. My body which had been cold for so long finally thawed out a little. Ant found a radio in the top pocket and switched on. Suddenly, the outside world was there again! "Hi Guys! How ya doin?" A voice boomed from the speaker. It would be a massive understatement to say that I was elated to hear another human voice. To know that someone out there is doing all they can to save your life is the greatest feeling you can ever have.

Ant talked to the pilot as I fumbled through the rest of the bag to see what there was. On the outside was a foam mat and I fully expected to find a tent and sleeping bags inside. I thought we would be spending another night on the mountain but I was wrong. The pilot had told Ant to get out the screamer suits. He had to refuel and would be back soon. We had to be ready for him. Screamer suits were the rescue harnesses designed to pull us off the mountain to safety. My hands were useless and Ant had to help me into mine. Because of the high altitude, we could only go one at a time. We decided that because of my hands, I would go first and he would follow on behind me. We dumped all our equipment and sat ready. I should have felt excited but still my mind was in a freezing nightmare.

Within minutes we heard the rotors and saw the helicopter rising once more. He hovered close and waved us over. I could see him struggling to hold her steady and a hurried feeling ran through me. Blasted by the freezing down draught, Ant helped me clip into the static line. It was one hell of a place to be – 20,000ft up with a struggling helicopter 30 ft above my head in a blizzard of ice. I held out my hand and screamed, "I'll see you down below Ant". We barely had time to shake hands before I felt a sharp tug and saw my feet leave the ground – I was airborne.

At first the ground dashed by me only a few feet below. I gripped the rope with all the strength I had and held on for grim death. I counted the height, one-foot, five feet, ten feet, thousands of feet. The ice disappeared as I left the plateaus edge and soared above the Genet Basin. Hanging thousands of feet in the air, suspended by a rope is hardly my idea of a joy ride but I didn't care. My fears disappeared, the cold faded and I let go of the rope. I forgot about my injuries and stared into the horizon. The sun was low and a crimson sky engulfed the mountains. It was a scene of stunning beauty which I will always hold in my mind. I heard nothing, felt nothing and flew like a bird over the mountains.

The joy ride came to an abrupt end. Within minutes I was down, unclipped, laid on a stretcher and rushed into a tent to wait for Ant. "Where's your third man? Where's your third man?" cried a voice. "Is he alright?" "He's up the mountain" I screamed as the helicopter blades blew powder snow everywhere and momentarily deafened us. There was nothing else I could say. As far as I was concerned, Steve had managed to get a rescue message through and was now alone on the mountain. Here I was at base camp again but in such different circumstances than three weeks before. All the hopes of the climb were gone and all I could think about was Ant, Steve and my battered body.

I felt a tugging at my feet as someone unclipped my crampons and then my harness. A voice whispered, "It's okay friend, we've contacted your family". My heart fell like a stone. How was I ever going to explain this to them? I was in the bloody mire this time.

A plane was waiting on the glacier to take us away. By now Ant had joined me and was able to walk onboard but I was stuck on my back. The flight seemed all of a daze but I do remember being strapped tightly to a stretcher and put inside the fuselage. That was about it. I never felt another thing until we hit the runway in Talkeetna. I know another plane took both of us to Anchorage but quite how and when is a mystery. It is said that we do not remember days, only moments. Well here was one of those moments.

Being strapped to a solid stretcher is damn uncomfortable. My back was in agony and I bellowed, "Will someone loosen these bloody straps!" I wasn't going anywhere unless the pilot wanted to suddenly loop the loop and I hoped he had no thoughts of that. Silently a hand appeared, unclipped the buckle and allowed my knees to bend.

My thoughts moved to Steve who was still up the mountain. He must have somehow got a message through and had saved us from a frozen death but he was now all alone and had to climb back to our camp, pack it up and descend to base camp before confronting his two friends in hospital. I pitied his situation before realising that I was in a much worse one myself. Here I lay injured but by how much I didn't know.

The flight must have taken an hour before we landed in Anchorage but still we weren't at the hospital. Across the field was a helicopter ready to fly us in. I have to say that the organisation was spot on - this was a practised evacuation, and one after another, Ant and I were wheeled into ER.

Suddenly, people started taking my clothes off. It felt so gentle and caring, quite a difference from the hustle and bustle of the flight. I had been transformed from the humming, shaking world of a small plane to the heavenly warmth and quiet of a hospital. Nurses busied around, taking blood pressures, cleaning me up and best of all, feeding me. I had forgotten how hungry and thirsty I was. I felt as though I could eat an ox and drink an ocean. Biscuits, sandwiches and hot drinks were held to my broken lips and I chomped and slurped them down furiously. My gloves and socks were slowly eased off and it became instantly obvious that I had severe frostbite. My fingers and toes were a dull yellow and began to throb incessantly, though I could not move or feel any life in them.

Though I could see all this happening, little registered in my mind. All I seemed to be concerned about was food and drink and having someone to talk to. Both hands and feet were plunged into a portable whirlpool bath and under its whooshing water some warmth slowly returned. The pain began to rise as my nerves thawed and regained consciousness. It was almost unbearable but I bit my tongue and silently held on. The throbbing seemed to run through my body and grasp at my soul. There was little I could do but keep my hands and feet in the whirlpool and pray it would all end.

The telephone rang - it was my sister. A nurse stuck the handset onto my shoulder and before I could string a few words together she was rattling down the line asking how I was. "I'm fine" I said "a bit battered but I'll be ok". I was lying through my teeth and I knew it. So did she. The tone of my voice gave it instantly away. I had no idea what on earth was going on or what would happen to me but it was wonderful to hear a homely voice again. Ant was only a couple of beds up from me. He was happy and joking and even took some pictures. I looked rough, bloody rough. My face was swollen, my body shattered and all my extremities held in the balance.

By now it was early morning. A trolley wheeled me off into intensive care where a dozen monitors were plugged onto my battered body. Out of the window, I could see a towering white mountain standing under a crimson sky. Some people may say that I needed to get away from the mountains but by now they were my home. I looked up at the clock. It was 4 am. I closed my eyes and within seconds, I was asleep.

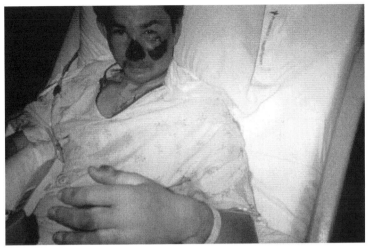

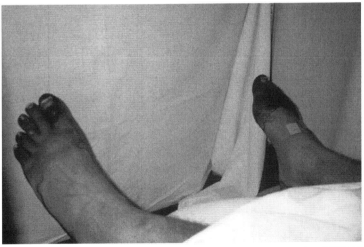

Day one in Hospital

CHAPTER 6

With a quiet creak the door opened and a shaft of light crossed the floor. I opened my dreary eyes and saw a silhouette enter the room. It walked towards me and said "Hi Nigel. How are you this morning?" I grunted some kind of response. "Fancy a bath and a shave?" It said. My heart leapt. At last a little luxury. I was lifted out of bed and transferred into a pool of warm water. Suddenly I felt my entire body relax. To feel the water running over my limbs was a true joy and I wanted to lie there for hours. My scrappy beard was silently cut away to reveal clean untouched skin underneath. I felt it with the back of my hand. It felt smooth as silk and homely. I was human once more.

My parents had telephoned to see how I was. I wanted to see them so much but hoped they wouldn't see me. The last thing I needed was them looking at their only son lying battered on a hospital bed. The press were pestering them night and day. I felt ashamed that I was putting them through so much but there was little I could do.

A procession of doctors saw me during that first day. It was thought that I would probably loose a toe or two but after that it was difficult to say. My heart fell. I felt my own mortality become a reality. No matter what the weather had done to me I didn't want to lose any part of my body but I had no choice. Whatever was done was done and nothing was going to reverse that. I stared blankly into the distance and said nothing for hours.

Ant dropped in later on to say hello. The lucky devil could walk around whilst I was stuck in bed. Envy ran through my bones. We had been there together in the same model boots, clothes and gloves, yet he had comparatively little damage compared to me. My left cheek looked as if I had been in ten rounds of a boxing match, my feet were elevated on pillows and my arms held in the air on slings. Lines sat in my spine and everything from my armpits down was a haze.

That evening I received a devastating shock. Steve had been brought in with severe frostbite and a broken leg. He had taken a huge fall but that's all I could find out. I thought he was still on the mountain getting the gear but something had gone badly wrong.

It would be five days before we saw each other again and through his smiling face, I could see the pain of his position. My injuries paled into insignificance against his. Steve's fingers were frostbitten to the core, his toes were beyond repair and one leg was braced externally with rods and bars. Incredibly he sounded alive and upbeat about it all – something I struggled to do. Though I didn't realise it at the time I was slipping into the deep valley of depression and I couldn't stop myself falling.

Later, I heard of Steve's rescue. A search team had found him lying in the snow nearly frozen to death. After he left Ant & I, he had descended the Washbourne Route but found no one. Climbing down Denali Pass he had taken a terrific fall. Most of his equipment had been lost and he had spent the night in a hole, scratched out in the snow. He was found the next day and flown in. I was so convinced he had contacted the rescue services who then picked up Ant and I. We had been warm in hospital whilst he had endured a lonely night out on the ice.

Although I have always believed in God, I never have been a churchgoing man. Something inside me wanted to pray. I couldn't believe that I could lose fingers and toes and called for help from above to shine down a light to help me.

Over the next few days I saw a change in my body. My fingertips became shrivelled and black. The tissue was truly dead. For some reason I didn't seem to worry too much, perhaps my sub-conscious mind knew it would come. Frostbite is like a creeping death moving silently over your skin. My feet looked better but were blistered badly and it wasn't until later that they succumbed to the dark spell. There was no return from this point on. I was losing tissue before my very eyes. The

Left foot after four weeks © 1999 NUH NHS Trust

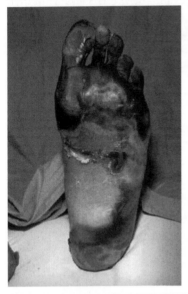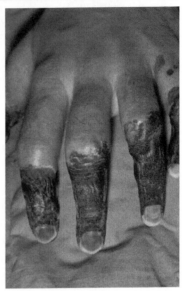

Left hand after four weeks © 1999 NUH NHS Trust

question was 'how much?"

It wasn't long before I had to face facts. My toes were dead and would need amputating. Tears ran down my face at the news but I couldn't wipe them away. My hands were still elevated. I was told that many people survived well without them but I didn't believe a word. I lay staring at their black form for days wondering if I would ever walk or run again. I had taken on the challenge of the mountain. Now it was having its revenge.

My sister Amanda flew over from England to be at my side. I had convinced myself that I needed no help but when I knew she was coming I couldn't wait for her to arrive. I can hardly describe my emotions when I saw her. I needed someone to talk to and someone to cry with. My strength had arrived and it showed. My mental state improved every day as we joked, told stories and toured the hospital together. I wondered what she felt for me at this time. Here she was, tending her only brother, as he lay useless on a bed with life changing injuries. I still looked a mess and thought what her first impressions were. She had seen me on TV but the reality of seeing me in the flesh must have been something altogether different. I don't think I ever asked her.

Talk began of sending us home. I felt unsure about the journey and if I would receive the same standard of treatment at home. Frostbite didn't seem a common injury for the UK but I was assured that a Burns Unit would be fine. Phone calls ricocheted across the Atlantic and the decision was made to send Steve & I to Nottingham City Hospital. Ant would go straight home. At least Nottingham was close to my home and the mental lift of having family and friends around would be better for me.

My epidurals were removed and I regained the feeling in my legs and lower body. Tingles ran down my nerves and muscles began to move again. This did bring one problem. Days of food were backed up and waiting for the green light. As feeling returned, my bowels began to rumble! I beat the call button with my elbow and screamed "Nurse, I need a bedpan now!" I was jacked up by my bum and dumped on the pan. It was the most undignified thing I had ever done but it was only the start. As soon as one pan was taken away, another was needed and I filled four in a row. The relief was wonderful and comic. Amanda and I boomed with laughter at my re-introduction to the toilet world.

The packing for home had begun in earnest. Bags lay everywhere full of medical supplies. They had even packed a bedpan. What will British Airways think of that? "Ladies and gentleman, we have just levelled out at 35,000ft. Our flying time is eight hours to London. Please clench your noses why the passenger in seat 56A takes a dump!"

Faces turned and stared when we entered the airport. Voices whispered as people gazed at this ungainly spectacle. We got onto the plane and began our journey home. It was painful, long and tiring. Flight connections were missed and arguments screamed across ticket desks but after 24 hours in plane and ambulance I lay in an NHS bed. I was only 20 miles from home. It might as well have been a 1000.

I was in a room and alone. It echoed with emptiness and had a cold, clinical feel about it. Disorientated as I was, it all seemed strange and though the travelling was over I still felt lost.

In was not long before my parents walked in. Their relief to see me safe and well was obvious but we struggled for conversation. The press had been giving them a hard time whilst I had been in Alaska. Their attentions now switched to the Burns Unit but they got little joy. Dad looked tired, Mum worried. None of us knew how long this was going to take. First estimates had thought weeks but now the impression was of months.

The door opened with a mighty clang at dead on 8am. "Good morning Nigel, time for your tablets!" The ward was up. I could see little through the door but heard the bustle of trolleys and bodies outside. Buzzers rang and voices echoed in the distance. Here it was a busier place than Alaska. It was a new routine to learn and plot into my mind. Bath time as was relaxing as ever and for once I was left alone to soak. These few moments were precious in my mind. Time to throw some of my inner thoughts outward and try to understand my perilous situation.

My arrival home had been well publicised in the press but as usual they got the story wrong. They made it sound like I was at deaths door. They wanted a story and if they couldn't get a good one they just made one up. It was here that I learned the phrase 'Never let the truth get in the way of a true story'.

Visitors were a welcome change but brought with them a bombardment of questions. "How are you? What happened? When is the surgery?" I realised that this was going to be the norm for the next few weeks as everyone came to visit.

The frostbite on my fingers began to peel away and revealed new skin underneath. The healing was working. All I had to do was keep the circulation going and hope for the best. I knew the recovery wouldn't be full but every little helped.

Vivid dreams of my past came to haunt me. I looked at my hands and saw long thin fingers but they faded away. I couldn't remember what they felt like before as the nerves were dead and gone. I looked at photographs of myself and focused only on the hands. Nothing else seemed to matter.

If you want to get known in the mountaineering world you have to do one of two things. Either climb something so ridiculous and groundbreaking that everyone stops and takes note, or be rescued in such a way that everyone hears about it. It seemed a sad reflection on life but true. How many athletes have run like the wind only to come second and be forgotten? Only if you break world records does anyone blink an eye and that's about all we do now. Gone is the world of massive first ascents that inspired a generation. Now we make a minute on the news and are forgotten.

I could not shake the fear of my surgery. How could I come to terms with losing fingers and toes? They are so small in relation to the body itself and yet so precious. Without them I would find life hard work. I could not imagine life without my 'little black bits' gone and stumps left behind. What would they look like after surgery? How would they work? How would I work?

The fingers were removed on my right hand first. After the operation sensation slowly began to return to my wounds. I felt a tingling in my palm and along my fingers but I knew they weren't all there. How could I feel anything? I dozed off and woke up with a start as I grasped my right hand. Everything moved with a sticky cold feeling. My finger ends leapt and my heart followed suit. I shivered for a few seconds then lay silent and still. How can I describe such a feeling? I didn't want to move anything because of damaging the skin grafts but needed to know what I had left. I felt around carefully trying to imagine where finger ended and reality began.

Days later the bandages were removed. Underneath laid a large pad draped over my palm. It was the last barrier between my eyes and the severed fingers I knew were waiting. The pad lifted slowly to reveal a messy stained hand, swollen and in pain. My fingers were short and looked butchered off. It was as if I had laid my hand out on a meat slab. Flaps of skin hung from the ends and stitches lay knotted in the iodine painted tangle. I stared trying not to believe what was before me. Silently I stared into the blackness of my mind somehow trying to comprehend the magnitude of it all. It was then the first tear rolled down my cheek, only to be followed by thousands more. I had become a freak, devoid of fingers and to be shunned from society. This was only the start. I had another hand and two feet to go.

People found it surprising how little Steve and myself saw each other. We talked for a few minutes each day but little more. People thought this very strange. Surely after such an experience we would be inseparable? We still had two separate lives to live with our own families. Yes, we shared our thoughts on the surgery and our different out comings, on the climb and what the future held but little more.

My hand shook as I gripped a pen and tried to write. It rolled around and skidded along the page with an alarming judder. Some was readable but most was a frantic scribble. All morning I sat and persevered. By dinnertime I was worn out but I had managed a few decipherable words and phrases.

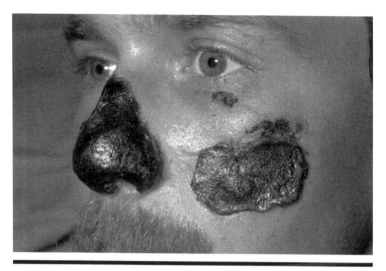

Koala nose and scarred cheek © 1999 NUH NHS Trust

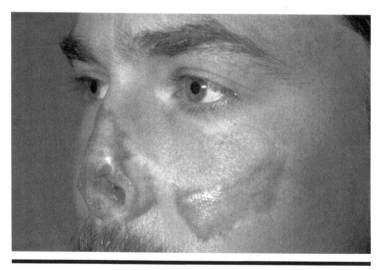

New Face - End of the Black Death © 1999 NUH NHS Trust

I began to write about the climb and my life since. It seemed to be a release from my thoughts of dread and horror at my predicament.

A vile smell began to rise from my nose. The necrotic tissue reeked of death and being so close to my nostrils it was impossible to get away from. Aromatherapy oils were used to mask the funk but it was no use. A young blond nurse hitched up her skirt and sat astride me in bed. Armed with a set of nail clippers she cut the loose tissue away. Other nurses stood ready to catch the skin as it ricocheted off the ceiling. The smell receded a little though I was just happy to have a nurse on my bed!

The morning of my second major operation I had a long conversation but not with a person. I sat in the bath and wished my remaining fingers and toes goodbye. Anyone watching might have thought me quite mad but they were old friends and we would never meet again.

Next thing I remember was lying in bed with people fussing around me. I felt dreadful. Nothing could describe the discomfort and pain of those next few hours. Both my legs from the knees down were numb. My left arm was numb. I thrashed about with my right trying to get comfortable but all I did was lose what little patience I had left.

Amanda held my hand as the bandages fell slowly from my feet. I had declined any pain relief preferring to bite on the agony and clear my mind. The padding revealed two stumps, lathered in iodine and rowed with stitches. They looked neat medically and that was what the nurses kept telling me. "They look really good Nigel". My eyes burned at their faces. "How the bloody hell would they know?" I thought. "Are they the one lying in bed carved in pieces?" It was a classic misinterpretation between us. They were talking medically of clean, well presented wounds in good condition, while I was thinking about my body and my future. I should have grasped the moment and said something but I didn't. My English resolve got the better of me and I stayed silent but fumed long into the night.

My left hand resembled my right. The meat cleaver had been struck across and chopped the dead tissue away. For the first time I couldn't cry. "You're so brave" I was told. Wrong. I was all cried out, there were no more tears to flow.

My legs had wasted away with inactivity. Being forced to lye in bed for weeks had robbed me of any muscle and strength. After losing my toes I had to walk but I didn't think these matchsticks could hold my weight. My feet were padded up and swung off the bed. I sat upright and felt my head begin to swim. I counted '1, 2, 3, go!' and pushed upward but nothing happened. I tried again and gave it everything I had. Slowly my legs straightened. I felt my spine buckle slightly but nothing was going to stop me from walking. I had to get upright again if my life was to improve. For days I had been telling myself to walk and convinced myself that I could do it but one fear had entered my mind. 'What if I fell over?' I wasn't worried physically; I just didn't want to make a fool of myself. Vanity had taken a hold of me.

The physiotherapists had brought a walking frame to help me but it was a bit short and I leant on it with a hunched back. Gently I pushed one foot in front of the other leaning on the frame in between. I can only describe the pain in one way; it was standing on a bed of razor blades but that wasn't going to hold me back. Once I start something I won't stop until it's done. "If you can manage a few steps that would be great" they said but I was determined for more than that. My blood was on fire and my mind focused on one thing and one thing only. I was going to walk and walk well. I shuffled towards the door when suddenly the frame was whisked away and I was on my own two feet. It was like the day your Dad took the stabilisers off your bike for the very first time. "If you fall over now we can't get you up. Hospital rules. We'd have to call an ambulance crew," they said. It was a great incentive to remain upright. This is where the word Physioterrorist comes from. They had lured me into a false sense of security and then outflanked me with a rapid pincer movement.

Onward I shuffled with a physio on each arm. 'If only I were fit and strong' I thought. 'I quite like having a young lady on each side'. We passed the door and entered the corridor. I amazed not only myself but also everyone else by the progress I was making. Rounds of applause were followed with "will you sit down! That's quite enough!" I had walked about twenty yards away from my bed but had to make the return journey in my wheelchair. I had stood tall for the first time in weeks and it felt good. My vanity was intact and I felt like a man again. I shook with emotion for hours and felt a little pride return. I had done it!

I walked more and more every day. It was all I looked forward to but at least I had something to hold onto. It still hurt like hell but that didn't matter. Being upright was more important.

Both my heels had been badly damaged and were not recovering well. My left heel bone was exposed and refused to mend. A VAC pump was attached. "What is that?" you may ask. Imagine this if you will. Take one Blue Peter presenter, a sheet of sticky back plastic, a length of clear plastic tube, a foam sponge and a vacuum pump. Fill the wound with foam, cover with the sticky back plastic, insert the tube into the foam and pump out the air. Sounds easy enough doesn't it? The problem was that it hurt like nothing before. The skin under my foot had come away from the bone and left a small void. A tiny strip of foam was delicately inserted four inches into my foot. It was like driving a knife in and turning it around just for fun. The advantage was that it speeded up the healing ten fold.

I left hospital after three months. This was by no means an escape but my life could begin to return to normal. I sat in my wheelchair staring at my own familiar hometown and noticed people looking at me. They never stared but squinted from the corner of their eyes. Children looked and were entranced by this 'Man in a pushchair' but their parents seemed to pull them away. We they embarrassed or was I that ugly? Conversations took place over my head on how I was or how the healing was going but few people actually talked to me. Instead they talked to whoever was pushing me. It was a strange feeling being there but not being involved the conversation. The welcomes were warm though and it felt good to be out in society once again. I had to make the most of every trip out because of my reliance on other people.

A slight cold was making life a little uncomfortable but it brought the end of the Black Death. I sneezed to find the last of my nose sitting in the handkerchief before me! It was over. All the dead tissue was finally gone. The surgeons couldn't get it loose but Mother Nature could. I almost felt sorry to see it go but realised I had a new nose. I stumbled into the bathroom and stared into the mirror. The tip had gone and my left nostril was short but I could breathe and feel free of the deathly scabs.

Winter came and I stood outside and felt soft snow melt on my face. The first falls were here and for me it was a special moment. These were the first flakes I had felt since McKinley. Memories of mountain views, cold mornings and hard climbs came and went in quick succession. It took a painful throb to break my strange dream. My hands started to ache with cold and I had to retreat inside to warmer climes. I hardly spoke a word all evening as my mind was completely transfixed by the weather. Nothing else mattered. Mountains do one of two things to you. Either you hate them forever, or you are totally transfixed. No matter what had happened to me I had to return back to the dizzy heights. I didn't know it then but it would be almost a year until I could climb again.

CHAPTER 7
RECOVERY

"Climb when ready!" screamed Ian. I felt the rope tighten but I still felt scared. "Are you coming or what?" "Climbing" I said. Stage fright had got the better of me. I was standing nervously at the bottom of Harboro' Rocks in Derbyshire attempting to climb in my new body. My mind was willing to go but my body had frozen. It was like the day I had climbed out of my hospital bed and walked over a year ago. I had spent months revving myself up for this moment and again I felt scared. Scared that I couldn't climb and scared in case I made a fool of myself. Here was my vanity rearing its ugly head again.

I put my hands onto the rock and felt it bite into my skin. It felt cold and damp but somehow homely. I moved my fingers around trying to find how best to hold this new surface.

Winter route in Torridon

Summit of Island Peak Nepal

There were no books to help me now. No trained medical staff to advise on a course of action. It was me and the rock. I gripped the best I could onto two small holds and thought "Sod it, here we go". I placed my right foot onto a large ledge and pushed. I jumped up and straightened my leg.

I was back on the face. Pain throbbed through my wounds as I stood there motionless. My feet were different sizes and I had struggled to get climbing boots to fit in any way, shape or form. Fortunately a shop sold me an odd pair, size five left and six right but I was still struggling. Climbing boots are pointed and close fitting but my feet were square and flat fronted. They had been nicknamed 'teddy bear feet'. It was not an ideal situation but like many so other parts of my life I had to adapt.

The sky was overcast and a chilling wind whistled round the hillside. Sixteen months had passed since my last climb and I felt relieved at being able to at least get off the ground, even if it was only two feet. I couldn't fall far as I was roped up but my wounds hated being knocked and I feared any slip would end in searing pain. You know that pain which never hurts straight away but after a second or two catches up with your nervous system and screams through your body like nothing else? Try stubbing your damaged foot into a rock and feeling what's left of your toe bones leap from under your skin. My fingers were masked under zinc tape but would suffer similar pain.

I suddenly became aware of the difficult predicament I was in. My hands were struggling to hold on and my feet were aching. They didn't reach the front of my boots so I had to stand sideways to get on the holds. After a few seconds everything began to throb. I had to move and get on with the climbing, not stand there thinking about it. I wedged my entire body into a large crack and pushed upward. I searched madly for a handhold but my fingers were incredibly fat compared to their length and I struggled to grip into the tiny cracks above me. Only two fingers on each hand were long enough to roll over the handholds easily, as all the others were tiny stumps.

I had been training hard in the gym for eight months for this day but I still felt weak. My arms began to shake and I could feel the muscles in my forearms pumping. I pushed with all my might and bared stabbing pain through both feet to reach a good handhold. I pulled myself up and within minutes I climbed my first route. It was a simple climb called Little Chimney which most climbers would use as a warm up but to me it was the start of my return to the climbing world. I leant back on the rope and was lowered slowly down.

A tingle ran through my entire body. I had done it. I had proved that I could still climb. I was shaking with a mixture of excitement and exhaustion but I didn't care. For those few moments I was the happiest man in the world.

I tried another couple of routes before my fingers felt sore and cold. Clouds were closing in and faint drops of rain were beginning to fall. It was time to retreat to the pub and celebrate. How do you describe the feeling of being able to climb again? All I can say is this. It had taken sixteen hard months to get that far and the fight wasn't over but I would never rest until I could climb freely on rock and ice again. I was determined to prove to both myself and everybody else that even after such a debilitating accident, if you have the drive and determination to keep going nothing will get in your way. I was on fire!

Two weeks later I was back at Harboro' complete with an audience and the BBC. They wanted to reenact my climb for the cameras and my family came to watch. It all felt a bit false making it look like my first climb but my experiences with the media made it an easy enough assignment. The cameramen didn't think so, particularly when we suspended one from a rope off the cliff tops. Well, he said that he wanted a different angle!

People congratulated me on my climb and many said

"Is that it then? You've proved that you can climb. Surely it must be time to retire?" I couldn't think of a worse thing to say. There is an old saying that 'if you fall off your horse, then you need to get right back into the saddle'. I had done that and there was no way in hell that I was getting out. I was sat firm in the saddle with both feet in the stirrups and aching to ride. It was tempting to go off and attempt something horrific but I took my time and worked on technique and strength. I had to learn what my body would do and how it would do it.

Winter came and I faced a new challenge. The cold. I was aching to climb on ice and snow but knew what it could do to my damaged hands and feet. Everyone seemed more scared than me at the prospect of winter climbing. Time and again I was told 'you must be mad' or 'don't be so stupid' but inside I knew what I wanted. My climbing friends were right behind me and so I took myself off to Scotland and faced the mountains of Torridon.

I had plenty of shiny new kit. All my original gear was still frozen high on the slopes of McKinley. My feet complained incessantly as I walked the two miles into the hills in new rigid boots. I had learned this was the only footwear that I could climb in but it was no good for distance walking. My feet didn't reach the fronts and my heels soon bled if I didn't mollycoddle them. My new ice axes were as yet unused and I wondered how I would be able to grip them en route.

Mentally I was better prepared and I reveled in the snows of winter. It was what I was born for. I sat and stared into the depths of the mountains. I was back at home in the placed I loved. I had missed it so much over the last couple of years and now I breathed in the cold air once more.

My feet complained at being strapped into crampons. They sat a couple of inches from the ends of my boots and so I kept rolling backwards. I retied the laces, tightened the straps and learned how to cope with this new balancing act.

I struggled to hold my ice axes for any period of time as my fingers ached. Swinging them into the face was difficult as losing my little fingers prevented any length of grip. I kept dropping them onto the leashes and picking them up again.

Through all this I never doubted my ability and used strength of will to climb. With help and encouragement I managed to ascend a 650ft route. My hands were freezing and my gloves were stiff. The snow had melted into them only to be frozen by the wind. They warmed up on the descent but my feet complained every step down. Back at the car park I inspected my heels. They were red and sore but intact. My hands were blistered but otherwise ok. I had nothing to fear. A few drams of whisky would soon sort everything out.

After that day I climbed more and more. I found it the release I needed to inspire me onwards in my life. I had already mastered skills like driving and even returned to work. Life began to return to normal and I found that I could do almost everything I had before. Yes, it was a little different but I had the drive to succeed. Tt was climbing however that got me out of bed every day. I set myself manageable goals and ventured across the world achieving them. I climbed in the Alps and Dolomites before the defining moment came in 2002 when I climbed Island Peak in Nepal. It allowed me to stand at 20,000ft again, the same altitude which had almost cost me my life.

It was by no means as technically difficult as Mt. McKinley but a massive personal challenge because of my injuries. The cold had bitten into my hands again but I escaped unmolested and stood in blazing sunshine on the summit. It was such a different place to Alaska. Here it was boiling hot and bright. Above me stood the mighty Lhotse and below were green fields and rock screes. Dozens of climbers were fighting for the summit but I felt alone. My mind was clear and my soul refreshed.

I walked down the glacier whistling away to myself before I screamed with joy as I eased my plastic mountaineering boots off my battered feet. They still suffered but had managed enough to get me to the top and back. I walked back to camp in trainers and spent a glorious evening watching the sunset across the mountains. My heart was full of emotion and my eyes were full of tears. From that day onwards I have never looked back and never stopped climbing.

It has been said that over the next few years I will always be "climbing another mountain", it being called Mt Recovery. The summit of this peak will be a full recovery from my wounds, both mental and physical. It is a vicious mountain to climb full of difficult sections which take every last scrap of energy you can muster to pass them. Days which become long and slow, suddenly burst into energy and then meander on at their snail like pace. It is a cold barren place to be, at times devoid of human life and feeling, empty and abandoned. Yet I will climb it and stand on that summit however high it may be and however long it takes. As with all climbs we struggle up the hardest sections for a few precious moments on the summit. Those precious moments are what keep me alive.

SECTION 2
WHAT I HAVE LEARNED

It would have been easy to end the story there but there is more to this tale than a climb. Through my experience I learned so much about myself and the world around me and I would like to share that knowledge with you.

CHAPTER 8
TRAUMA

If you want a true meaning for Trauma open a dictionary. It's listed as a 'deeply distressing experience, physical injury or emotional shock following a stressful event'. Been there. Done that. Got too many scars but don't wear the t-shirt anymore. Trauma isn't something we just see on TV shows but a real emotion, which changes lives.

I found the most obvious effects were the physical ones. Frostbitten tissue is black, hard and withered. It looks like an Egyptian Mummy and feels cold and morbid. It stands out to everyone who sees it, and initially I found it embarrassing to show. I felt safe in the bounds of the ward but my parents took me out of hospital one afternoon as a treat. I had to lie across the back seat of the car before shuffling out into my wheelchair and facing the world. I was covered in a thick woolen blanket, even though the day was hot. I wore a large hat and tried to hide in my wheelchair. Why? Because I didn't want to frighten anyone. It was my first time in public and my frostbitten fingers and toes were still attached. My nose was black and a deep scar sat on my left cheek. I thought of myself as ugly and repulsive to other people. "Who would want to see such a horrible thing?" I thought to myself, even though I was desperate to get out, if only for a few hours. I shunned eye contact and hoped no one would notice me but it was a Sunday and Wollaton Park was busy. Some people recognized me and wanted to say hello. I had been in the local news and was apparently quite a celebrity. They were inquisitive about my wounds and just wanted to chat. It was all very innocent but a great lesson to me in human understanding and reality. I have no idea who those people were, but I thank them from the bottom of my heart.

Over time my inhibitions faded, although I did cover my wounds when my young nephews came to visit. They had an idea of what had happened to me and had probably seen pictures on TV but I felt the real thing was perhaps a little too much for them. They were only 7 and 12 years old at the time.

What I did discover later on is that children find my wounds fascinating. This showed me how trauma affects different people of different ages in different ways. I have lectured many times about my injuries and always find the youngsters want to see the gory photographs whilst many adults turn away. Children love them! Some ask to touch my hands and face to feel what the wounds are like. One asked me if he could see my feet and within moments I was standing barefoot before a group of teenagers.

The frostbite on my feet prevented me from walking for weeks. Physically that is a great loss to the body. My legs began to fade at an alarming rate and the Physio's did all they could to help me keep some muscle tone. Weights were strapped around my calves and I would sit in bed for hours doing reps. I just wanted to do anything to keep them in shape. I did similar exercises with my arms but it was hard to keep any real strength. When you are immobile, your whole body begins to change. All that muscle you spent years building soon fades and even now I have never got it all back. My amputations meant that tendons were moved around during surgery and my muscles cannot rebuild. Sounds bad doesn't it? Actually it isn't. I still cycle, walk in the hills and climb across the world. Things are different and there are no straight answers to how your injuries have affected you, but if you are prepared to work hard with them, you can rebuild your life.

Losing my fingers also brought massive changes to my life. People said that I would not climb again, or even live without specialized help but I have proved them all wrong. Things are different and I cannot do everything I once did with my hands. Such examples are opening anything with a ring pull. Thousands of beer and food tins come fitted with them these days. I have to lever them open with a tablespoon and just get on with life. You would have to put a much harder task before me to separate me from beer. Few people actually notice my missing fingers because I do everything they do, without a hitch. I have had to change a few things around the house such as tin openers and scissors but that's all.

One of my biggest worries was if I would still be able to shoot. Fingers are vital when there is a trigger to pull and I was forced to change guns. With some professional help I have mastered a new grip and I'm now I'm as good a shot as I ever was.

Being bed bound made me feel like some kind of Robinson Crusoe, abandoned on my island of metal and blankets over a sea of linoleum. I escaped via my wheelchair occasionally but needed help to embark and paddle. Though I do enjoy solitude, too much can be dangerous, particularly when you are injured and vulnerable. Staff, friends and family alike did their best to help but windows can be dangerous to stare through with an empty mind and a blank face.

Suicide is not a subject to write easily about. I've seen people joke about it and it makes me sick. I stared too long out of the windows in hospital when very vulnerable and I seriously considered ending it all. I was in pain and discomfort and the surgery had been so severe that I just wanted a quick way out. Lying there alone I felt pitiful and sad. I was feeling sorry for myself and my mind going downhill fast. I stared outside knowing that I was two floors up and the drop was onto solid concrete. It seemed a quiet and unassuming way to go. What I hadn't comprehended was this. I couldn't move due to ample anesthetic and the window wouldn't open. These were major problems. More importantly was the fact that if I ended my life then I would be affecting the lives of so many others, particularly my families. Suicide can be a selfish way to end your problems. Having seen at first hand what it does to other people I would not recommend it. Think carefully about what is happening to you.

I can't run much and though I still walk in the hills, I cannot do the distance I once did but I'm happy. My speed is a little slower but I still get wherever I'm going. This was one of the hardest things to face, but I have, and live everyday as if there was never ever any change.

Rock climbing isn't what it was but I have moved my expectations and now enjoy more scrambling in Wales, The Peaks and the Lake District.

This brings in an interesting point – moving expectations. Don't get this confused with lowering them. They are two very different things. There were things I just had to admit that I would struggle with after surgery.

Driving brought a new feeling to my life, or should I say took one away. You see when I first sat in the driving seat I realized one thing – I couldn't feel the pedals. I had shoe there, but the rest was, and still is guesswork. When I pushed down, I had to work out where my foot was in relation to the pedal and hope that I could feel resistance. It was a hard lesson to earn, particularly with a car under your control.

This feeling came to me in many other parts of my life – I could see a shoe pushing, but there was no foot there. Stiffness of shoes and the amount of grip they had all became new concerns for me. I can now just jump into the car and go but it took time to realize that I was pushing something that I couldn't feel, with nothing. Memory plays a great part here in keeping you above water. I know people who can't feel their hands and feet through diabetes and they live a similar experience to me. You can see it's there but not feel a thing. This can of course be dangerous, but thankfully I passed my driving test without a hitch, so all road users beware!

Physical change soon breeds frustration. Active people don't celebrate when told to sit down and do nothing for three months. We make bad couch potatoes. I fidgeted and played in an attempt to break the restrictions of my injuries but my efforts were to little avail. The human body will only work at one pace – its own. No matter how much I wanted to walk or move I couldn't. Not until my body let me. I had grown up in a world of engineering where timetables and plans were set down and worked to. There had been little room for delay and charts showed progress and projection. My mind wanted to do the same with my body. It needed projected timescales and progress meetings to monitor itself but they did not exist. It took weeks before I finally closed these feelings down and let nature take over. We live in times which revolve about timescales and performance. Work drills this into many with great vigor but blood vessels, muscle tissue and skin cells don't recognize performance related targets.

Physical immobility brings with it problems in controlling body weight. I put on over three stone in three months and felt like a beached whale. I didn't protest as I was under orders to eat a high protein diet and keep my body's fuel tanks topped up. Large meals, snacks and protein drinks were poured into me with inevitable consequences, but you can't build a house without the correct materials.

If any of you have been in hospital you may have seen the menus, which are brought round the day before for you to choose from. If I didn't tick enough boxes, the nurses would and did feed me the extra. I had to throw my vanity aside for a while to allow recovery to take place before I could begin to get back into my trousers.

People moan about NHS food but I found it ok. There is nothing to beat your mums cooking when you get home though. Thankfully by then I was a little more mobile but it wasn't until I got back on my feet fully that I returned to my original weight. Talking of which, Steve came over one day for a chat. He was on full-length wooden crutches due to a lower leg amputation. He sat down and told me the story of his weight problems. He was losing where I was gaining. "I've lost three quarters of a stone and I don't know why" he said. Instinctively we both looked at where his left leg once was and roared with laughter. Talk about wood and trees! Now my diet is as normal as anyone else's but I do take care due to bowel problems. Medication masks pain but can bring with it unfortunate side effects.

Pain is an inevitable part of trauma. Physically you feel it rolling about your body in an uncontrollable turmoil but modern drugs help. The epidurals in Alaska knocked everything out but they were short term and so tablets took over. Thirteen every morning for breakfast and so on. Pain one of the greatest fears in life. I have a reasonably high threshold but over time it wears even me down. Amputations can cause shooting pain, making you jump; where as muscular pain makes you ache. Before surgery I was physically ok but afterwards I had some bad days. Cutting nerve endings, however dead brought nights of discomfort and fear. It was like being a child again and suffering horrific nightmares but there was little chance of sucking my thumb.

Few people like pain, I certainly don't but it is part of life and we have to face it. Distraction is a great help; anything which can take your mind away, if even for a few moments, is good. I suffered real pain in my heels. The left was stripped to the bone, and for the first time in my life I saw the inside of my body. There was my heel bone, exposed to the world and looking dull grey. It was scraped until it bled and fitted with a vacuum pack to draw out the tissue. I wore this for a few weeks and it did a great job. The dressing was changed weekly and packed with special foam. During the week my nerves and blood vessels grew into this. Imagine the feeling when that was pulled out. It was one of the few times I almost screamed.

New nerves don't like being banged or stubbed and even now my feet are tender but again I strap on climbing boots and head for the hills. Finding people who will help with shoes and boots was vital, and it took some doing. At first they were lost about what to do as I was such a strange case but together we worked hard and I have freedom again to walk and climb.

Physical pain is one thing but mental pain is another. Watching your body die before your eyes is the most painful thing I have ever had to suffer. There is nothing you can do but wait, believe in the Doctors, and pray. Frostbitten wounds turn from red to purple, and then to black. Hair and nails still grow but the tissue is dead. No matter how ugly they look and how dead they are, they are still part of you and you don't want to lose them, but you have little choice.

Physical scars heal in time with care and treatment but mental scars need special help. My surgery took place over a number of weeks and I lost my right fingers first. As I mentioned earlier in this book, I sat in the bath at six am one morning and wished them goodbye. Who do you know who walks to their hands? It wasn't madness or delusion that made me do this, more the fact of wishing some old friends goodbye forever. That moment has become one of the special memories which has been etched into my mind. No amount of professional help can ever begin to understand what I was going through at that time but I just had to do it.

Tablets remove both mental and physical pain, because they can. Chemicals react with the body to the desired effect and cure everything from headaches to malaria. Physical scars will rebuild themselves and then no help is needed but I do fear being on medication for mental scars. I had a little to start with, but they stopped after a few weeks and I was very happy about that, because the only way to face pain is head on and using your own strength and energy. I won't hide behind a mask of chemicals. Many in society use drugs and alcohol to take away the pain and I find that incredibly sad. I don't deny that for some a short-term prescription is needed to get them through a rough period but the only person who can get over whatever it is, is you. It might sound all a bit macho but in my view it is the truth. If you want something badly, such as mental peace, you have to fight for it. Taking drugs is only a delaying action to facing the truth, however unpleasant that is.

Crying is something we don't do enough of as men. We're far too hard for that, aren't we? I don't think so. Why do we have this compulsion that crying makes us weak? Is it something which we learned as children in the playground? "Crying's for girls!" was screamed often enough as I remember. I bawled my eyes out on a regular basis as I lay in bed and even now I shed a few tears. They may be in private but I think they are the sign of a real man rather than some weakling. Trauma is played out on a level field and we are all the same when injured. Reality hurts and there is no shying away from it.

Trauma affected one very personal part of my life – relationships. I just couldn't understand how anyone would ever want to love me. "Who would want to look at me?" I used to think to myself. I thought I was ugly and disfigured and convinced myself that no woman would cast her eyes on me again. Thankfully I was wrong. It did take a couple of years for me to gain the courage to ask but eventually I managed it. I found some advantages – many women find men's toes the unsexiest part of the body. I was in there! I struggled to undo buttons and so she had to undress me. Bras were a nightmare but they are to most men.

What I feared the most was the ability to touch and feel. After having my fingers removed I had little sensation in my hands. I stroked her skin but struggled to feel anything. Over time some sensation returned and I could once again feel her body. My nerves would jump with excitement every time this happened because I thought it had gone forever. My sense of smell was so bad that when I brought perfume I almost had to almost snort the bottle and I had hours of fun at the counter!

She was compassionate and loving towards me and did more for my state of mind than all the physiotherapists in the world put together. It only lasted a few months, but it brought me out from the emotional wilderness.

I've talked enough about myself but this adventure was not taken alone. Steve and Ant were with me and I think it's important to bring them in here. It's all to easy to talk endlessly about yourself as an individual but here were the two people who went through frostbite with me, although to different physical effects.

Ant didn't stay in hospital with Steve and I. He was allowed home as soon as he touched British soil. At the time I thought he was lucky but there is always the fear of being forgotten when you are not at the centre of attention as Steve and I were. The physical injuries were different but the mental ones were connected. At least Steve & I had the hospital staff to support us. I felt that Ant had been put out to pasture and had to deal with everything without specialist help. He did have the freedom to roam though and I was jealous of that.

Though Steve and I were in the same ward we rarely saw much of each other. Why? Because we were in separate rooms and both bed bound. Looking back it would have been a great help if we could have talked more about our personal experiences at an early opportunity but we didn't. It wasn't until later on that we got any chance of that. The two most injured people were kept apart and in my opinion that was a great lost to both of us. When people of similar experience can talk, so much can be understood without explanation.

Since then we have all kept in touch and I have noticed how our lives have changed due to the trauma we suffered. Families have parted and relationships changed but as far as I'm concerned that's all water under the bridge. Trauma doesn't just affect the casualty but also the family and friends which surround it. Many struggle to cope with watching a loved one suffer before their eyes, or worry about how their life will change but in the end we are still the same people however we look or feel.

Having limbs amputated is not only painful but also obvious to everyone around you. Those tiny parts of your body, so small in percentage figures against your whole, make such an incredible difference to your life. Size does not always matter.

CHAPTER 9
SURVIVAL

The art of survival has a massive part to play in my story. After all, if I hadn't survived, I wouldn't be writing this book. Survival isn't just about training, skill and knowledge, but also luck and the effects of others around you. Instinct plays a part, but being prepared is vital. Having the correct equipment or provisions to survive makes a massive difference to your chances. It's a huge subject, which has been popularised by television and the media. Many people talk to me as if they have been out in the wilds for years, but few have, or would even dare to go.

It doesn't matter how much training you have in life, there's always room for more. For years I had trained and survived in jungle, high altitude and snow conditions across the world before flying to Alaska, and so I felt well prepared. I had taught expedition skills for Raleigh International and been on many independent courses myself; always learning that little bit more. I loved building jungle camp from a few tarpaulins, sleeping in a hammock and cooking over an open fire. Winter camps are different, but living in tents, eating food cooked over a petrol stove and sleeping on ice is just as good. Water, food, fire and shelter are the main needs in our lives and as long as we have them then all is fine. I use the word needs here, as survival is not a subject that includes wants. You can live quite well without wants, but we choose not to because of comfort, convenience and keeping the family happy.

I'm not going to say I was an expert, but you cannot do your job well if you haven't been trained to do it, and climbing is no different. Life is full of examples, good and bad. Most of us have probably sat a driving test. That nerve-wracking hour seemed like a week, but would you have passed it without those long arduous lessons? Probably not. It's a very simple example I know, but it highlights the point. There are the extremes though.

I was once invited to a session, in a modern office building, on how to climb the stairs from reception to the first floor. The reason was because someone had fallen down them. I found the reason they fell was due to poor footwear and chatting on a mobile telephone, not lack of training. Climbing stairs is one of the myriad lessons we learn as children and we do it naturally and without a thought. Yet, the company thought it a good idea to show everyone how to climb them. I think reality has to take a hand here so as not to offend too many people but really, how far do you take it before insulting intelligence?

Risk is an inevitable part of life. In my opinion we live in a society obsessed with it to such a point that living itself is threatened. This is particularly well highlighted in our children's lives. Schools ban games such as British Bulldog and cut down trees to prevent them being climbed. There always seems to be some do-gooder wearing a killjoy hat to stop children having fun. I'm not saying that falling out of trees isn't dangerous, of course it is, but unless you allow children to realise risk at an early age, what hope do they have as they grow older? Where do they learn the boundaries of risk? It must be in childhood and not read from theory or computer projection. As a boy I regularly played soldiers in the woods and got covered in dirt, stung by nettles and shot at my friends with a cap gun. What would people think?

The mountains are an environment filled with risks such, as avalanches, crevasses and bad weather but that doesn't stop people venturing into them. Many are injured, or even die, but year after year people return because they are a place of excitement, challenge and beauty. As climbers we assess risk at every second and make decisions which can affect the lives of many but we do it subconsciously. It used to be called common sense, but that seems to have been thrown out of the window these days. I would dread to think of a group of safety bods sat at base camp with their manuals and laptops. "Have you completed a risk assessment before you leave your tent?"

they would be saying. "You can't go out there. It's below the statutory working temperature for this environment". Go get a life, and keep out of mine. I accepted the risks that climbing McKinley would bring and I paid the price, but I don't sit here moaning about it. I'm hardly going to sue the mountain for negligence.

On that point, I was in my wheelchair in town one morning when a young chap in a sharp suit approached me. He was looking for people who had suffered "an accident in the past three years" and must have noticed me a mile away. "That looks nasty sir," he said. "Was anyone else involved?" "Yes, two others" I replied. His eyes shone like dinner plates and pound signs chinked into place. He though he was onto a winner. "Was anyone to blame sir?" "Only the weather." "Where were you sir?" "At the top of a mountain in Alaska". His face fell instantly. He wished me a good day and left me with a smile beaming from my lips. I cannot stand vultures that prey on the injured or weak. If there is real negligence then fine, but otherwise forget it. In my view they are surrounded by too many wants, and not enough needs. The claim culture we live in seems to me to be obscene. Should we be making money out of other people as if it is a pastime? It is a sad reflection upon society when the first words after an accident are not "Are you alright?" but "You'll be hearing from my solicitor!"

Teamwork is paramount to survival. As human beings we survive much better together, than if alone. We can save energy as a team if shelters need building, food cooking and bodies warming. When you're shattered after a hard day climbing every calorie is important. Splitting up the workload speeds things up no end and when it's blowing a blizzard you can't get into your tent fast enough. Also if the chips are down it's always good to have someone to talk to. It's possible that I wouldn't have made it off the mountain without Ant's help, as talking kept me awake and alive. If you feel abandoned, you will abandon yourself and that starts a deadly spiral of depression that can lead to death.

Teams can be too large, particularly when cramped into a mountain environment and I find three or four people plenty. In the jungle larger numbers are ok as there is more space to spread out. Personal space is important but working together well can make the difference between success and failure, or life and death. I try to share this ethic with the business world but teamwork isn't just about working together in business, sport or leisure. It extends into our personal life too. Families make wonderful teams, if fact my Dad and I have worked together as a two-man team for years. It all started because he didn't have a gundog but he had a young son who could run and fetch and thought it wonderful to be out with him. We have worked together ever since on all kinds of projects, to the point that we know what the other is thinking.

Sharing is also part of survival. Sharing the climbing, workload, weight and responsibility is vital in the mountain environment. Some people will carry others, others want to be carried but generally the weights balance out. No one slackened on our trip because there was no capacity to but in large groups there will always be one or two who try. There are some who will not share though. I've known people hoard food from others even when they see them starving, and almost enjoy the experience. Others will hide things away and deny their existence just so they can have whatever it was. That kind of attitude will get us nowhere. I've given people my food, climbing gear and even money before to get them out of a tricky situation, and all I ask for is a thank you. If I don't get that then words will be said. It's all well and good wanting but manners cost nothing. Sharing isn't just a physical thing as we also share stories, jokes, information and knowledge.

Knowledge gets us through life. We need to know what's happening everyday in our lives and how to deal with it.

Everything from how to dress, start your car and ride the surf is attained by knowledge. The mountains are no different. We can learn from books or the Internet, but good old fashioned first hand experience is the best.

We had all climbed and travelled across the world and practised together at home as a team, but three skilled climbers who know everything but can't work together would have been useless. It sounds like some places I have worked in over the years where people don't get on. They are all pulling in opposite directions, getting nowhere but expending energy doing it. Sound familiar? Sharing knowledge is one of the greatest things you can ever do. Ant helped me cook at altitude and Steve helped with the technical climbing stuff. We can learn so much just by sharing our knowledge and not treating whatever we know as some kind of Black Art. I find learning from theory ok but learning from others is much quicker and more enjoyable.

Of course it's all right having all this knowledge but do you have the skills to use it? Some people soak up information like a sponge but can't put it to use. Others have little academic skill but can build anything you like using a pencil scribble and a pile of bits. We all know our skills, or we should do. Opportunity to use them properly is the problem.

My hands make things like woodwork a little harder for me these days, but I still do it. In fact one of the first jobs I did after recovering was helping my Dad build a wooden conservatory. I dropped dozens of screws and covered myself in cuts but two days later it stood finished. I had to change a few tools, and realise that I was a bit slower than before. Here I was moving my expectations again and still using my skills. It was another milestone in my recovery and in two days I learned what some take years to digest.

I was thankful of the woodwork shop back in hospital. They brought people together who had all manner of injuries to share experience and skills, talk and make friends. I cannot rate an experience like that highly enough. After suffering injuries such as mine, the opportunity to build something useful was too important to miss. Did your Grandmother ever have one of those stools which had a wound string seat? Well I made one and still use it to plonk my feet on in an evening. Lacing the seat taught my hands how to grip and began bringing bank the strength in my fingers.

Before the trip I had spent months badgering businesses at home for good equipment. The choice seems endless these days and you need experience to wade through the piles of stuff that isn't up to the job. We are surrounded by tons of 'Made in China' gear which in my opinion isn't the best. It fits a targeted market and that's that. I'm not saying that there's anything wrong with it but I do question the 'made for £30, sold for £300' ethic. I have always tried to buy gear made in the UK but that's very hard. Most of the stuff I managed to get was British made and worked very well. If anyone says "It can't be that good as you all got frostbite" I will say only this. You go and sit at 20,000ft in -60C and lets see how you feel. I can't stand Armchair Adventurers who have opinions based on little more than pictures and television shows. They get right under my skin. Anyway, let me get back to gear before I lose it completely. Equipment for anything has to be fit for purpose, used correctly and be in the environment it was designed for – you don't wear down jackets on the beach in summer! We had great equipment which was designed for the mountains and did its job well. That's all you can ask of it but that's ok if you know how to use it. Here's knowledge again. Can you put your tent up in a gale or blizzard? Do you know how to light your stove in the wind? All these questions need to be asked and solved long before you even set a foot on the plane.

I think that luck has its part to play in survival. With good luck on your side you can escape from anywhere but if bad luck overcomes you, you are doomed. When being interviewed by the press I was often told, "you were very lucky to get out alive". Indeed I was but there is more to it than that.

Luck can be due to many things but one is the correct order in a chain of events. Things happen in life all the time, and if they happen in the correct order you are lucky and in my case saved. If the helicopter had come earlier or later in the chain, I might not have made it. In everyday life that chain works the same but the failure of one link will break the chain. Things such as breakdowns, accidents and missed appointments throw peoples lives into turmoil. What once seemed so planned and simple suddenly collapses around them. "The best laid plans of mice and men" and all that. The chain is not purely coincidental. Other people play a massive part in it and they are beyond your control. Luck guides them towards you on a collision course and their impact may have wonderful or catastrophic consequences. Think about a relationship you may have had. Were you at that party, that night and met that person? That meeting was the chain of events working. If you had been at another place the same night at the same time, you still may have met someone, but someone else. The lasting and loving relationship will be built on the links of correct chain.

Weather has a massive part to play in my story. The cold almost killed me but the break in the clouds saved me. So much media attention is focused on the weather. It can bring beauty and light, or disaster and death. In the climbing world it is a long talked over subject. Summit days, rest days and retreats are all weather related. The exposed positions we put ourselves in demand absolute attention to detail. Thick cloud not only obscures the view but also brings rain and snow. The avalanche risk can then heighten and a retreat to safer climbs may be necessary. Deep snow makes the going hard and cloaks crevasses under its thick blanket. It may look beautiful but it's just waiting for you to venture into it. I've been in situations where wind and rain have smashed jungle camps to the floor and a speedy move needs to be made. People, equipment and stores must be hastily moved in foul conditions but you have little choice. Weather can force you into tight corners where snap decisions are needed and they can mean the difference between life and death. The learning possibilities here are endless and boys become men overnight.

Years ago in Chile I had to evacuate a seaside camp from the shore, as the spring tide came higher and higher. Alongside me was James, a 17 year old who I thought looked a bit fresh faced. How wrong I was. He worked quickly and was mature, thoughtful and good at decision-making. The jungle became our home with beds in the trees or on deep moss. Between us we saved eight people and almost the entire camp. They moaned like hell because their sleep was disturbed, but would they rather have drowned? In one evening a great friendship was formed through the world of survival. The best bit is sitting down afterwards with a cup of tea in your hand and a wry smile on your face.

I regularly climb in Scotland and face the winter winds over the Cairngorm Plateau. They are strong, biting cold and energy draining. They remind me of McKinley. Wind is a real killer. It can blow you off a mountainside or freeze you to death, yet we think little of it. It's only when it hits the news that many take notice. Wind is what turns snowfall into blizzards and rain into monsoons. Weather is a combination of nature's forces working together in a delicate balancing act.

In connection with weather come atmospherics. The small handheld radios we had in Alaska struggled to make communication with Base Camp. They were underpowered and relied on line of sight, so why were we given them? I don't know, perhaps cost or availability? What I do know is that voice communication was impossible, but there are many types of communication in this world. The atmospherics might have been against us but a message got through and we were saved. That's enough for me. I have used radios across the world with varying success and sounded like a Dalek on many occasions but it is something you get used to. Do we expect too much of the world of communications? My view is yes we do. Any interference sends people off in a frenzy of complaints but when nature changes its atmospheric abilities, there is little anyone can do. The sun causes entire communications blackouts when a burst rises from its surface. It is something we didn't need to worry too much about years ago as there was little to affect but now life is a different matter.

I wrote earlier that survival is not always down to just you, but can involve other people. The Rescue Services, Medical Staff and your Family all have their part to play. Sometimes they play a forgotten role, often shunned by the press and largely ignored. I feel that is a disgraceful state of affairs, as these are the people who give you your life.

I can't thank Jim Hood enough as he was the pilot of the Llama Helicopter which took me off the mountain. Working with Daryl Miller and the Denali National Park Service he brought me down to base camp and allowed me to live again. The press made much of the rescue at the time, mainly due to its heroics and unfortunately, politics. There was an argument going on about whether foreign nationals should be rescued for free off American soil. We offered to pay but no one wanted our money. The rescue services were forgotten later on and that has caused insult and irritation ever since. These special people put their own lives at risk and deserve a special mention.

There are many people in the same position such as Lifeboat Crews and Mountain Rescue Teams. Few wish the media spotlight but recognition of their efforts is both respectful and decent. I was at a Queen and Paul Rogers Concert in Hyde Park only a few days after the London Bombings of 2005 and found it heart-warming that people from the emergency services had been given free tickets. A little recognition goes a long way.

The hospital staff from both Anchorage and Nottingham continued where the rescue services left off. They rebuilt my life and helped me come to terms with my injuries. I was very macho at first and thought I could manage but again I was wrong. I needed help and was too proud to ask. Eventually I did, and even now I'm still benefiting by their guidance.

Survival isn't just about getting through the experience and going home. It's a personal journey through life for many, and I've found surviving the long-term injuries harder than surviving the mountain.

Surviving at home was a great test for me. We get used to our surroundings and know what is kept where and in which cupboard but imagine not being able to lift a saucepan or fill the kettle. This was survival in a new field for me. I was so used to lashing ropes and building bivouacs that the simple things passed me by. Don't get lost in SAS manuals or television shows. For many, survival begins in the home. Holding a cup was a test all on its own, never mind cutting my food. Putting on clothes, brushing my teeth, tying my shoelaces – all were survival techniques I had to learn again. I was determined to pass all these trials and live my life without permanent help and found great help within my family and the therapists in hospital. People will always make their own assumptions about you, and I'm forever asked what it's like to live in the wilds. No one ever asks me what its like to take my shoes off after a hard day, or how it feels to fight with the small change in my pocket. These everyday tasks are as much a part of my survival now as anything I have done overseas. It's all down to proportion and perspective.

Mental survival denotes your character and personality. The way you survive in life will dictate how you live it and how other people react to you.

So there you have it. Survival enters every sphere in

our lives. We all have the knowledge and skills to survive but many are dictated by the surroundings we live in. It is when we leave these that the real survivors will shine through and lead, where others will follow.

CHAPTER 10
TRUTH & HONESTY

It does depend on your point of view, but in my world there are sides to every story. Yours, mine and the truth. Lets be honest here, no matter what we say about something, someone else will have a slightly different opinion. Look at the daily news. Ten people will give ten differing accounts of the same incident, and all are correct. What we need to ensure in all this is honesty. Are we being honest with ourselves and others when we describe and live our lives? Steve, Ant and I all have our accounts of what happened up on the mountain, and if you were being picky, you might find slight differences in them, but we are all honest in our views. The difference is opinion and the angle from which we experienced it and saw it happen. I'm going to try and explain my views on truth and honesty together, as they are difficult, if not impossible to separate.

Dishonesty in not welcome in my personal world. If you are dishonest then you are living in a dream and lying to yourself, and what's the point in that? It is childlike to believe anything else, as the world will soon find you out if dishonesty enters your life. I had to be bluntly honest with myself during my recovery. It was obvious that things had changed, but I wasn't sure by how much. It would have been easy to say that I was fine and that everything was ok, but it wasn't and I had to face it. Decisions are easy to put off or delay when you don't want to face them. We do it all the time in our lives at home or work, because it's easier to put things off than face reality. They can be hard to deal with or to live with, but we have little choice if we truly believe in honesty, and after all, it's the best decision in the long run. If you were in a bad relationship or a job you hated, would you keep putting off the decision to leave through fear or apathy? Many do, but you are lying to yourself more and more as time goes on. The longer you wait the harder it is to make the right decision. Some learn this delaying tactic at an early age, but if you start off badly then the rest of your life will be tainted.

At first being honest physically was easy for me. It was obvious what my problems were as people could see my injuries for themselves, and I had little to explain. What was difficult was being honest when it came to doing tasks that I had once taken for granted. I have talked about some earlier in this book, such as driving, but there were things which I could not do once my fingers were gone. It was time to face reality and ask for help. Packaging is a nightmare for me, and I miss my fingernails when it comes to opening food and drink. A large knife helps, but it does scare people when I meet them at my door! How many times have we felt similar feelings? No, not the knife, but the fact that things in our lives have changed and we need to be man enough to ask for help. We men believe in being hard and tough, and not having to ask your mum to help you out when you are 30 years old. Many struggle to ask for even the smallest thing because we feel that it will destroy our image, and we will lose face. I can tell you right now that all that is rubbish. If you need help then ask. You would if you were on a sinking ship and couldn't swim. Be honest with your feelings and let people into your life to help you. It's a massive step to take, but many are just aching for you to ask, before they leap into action.

I could have easily given in to a word that I detest – convenience. I was surrounded with catalogues offering all kinds of gadgets to help me get over my injuries and live my life. You may have seen them yourself. Kitchen aids and hundreds of things to help you dress come to mind. For many they have good uses as they may be old or infirm, but I was determined not to give in! I was 30 years old and not some Granddad of 90. I kept getting asked "what about this to help you pick up the kettle" and the like. I rebuffed all attempts at gifts and got on with my recovery. I would decide what worked and what didn't. Many people think they are helping you by pushing in, but they are not. I asked everyone to bear with me, as I would ask them if I needed help. People said I was lying to myself, but I wasn't. I was being very truthful. I put the effort in and got the reward out. Because of this I manage to live my life normally. If you give into convenience you will become used to it and depend on it. In my view that is no way to live your life. Look at the world we have created. Convenience in time, travel, money and manpower is killing us all. If we believe that we can go on as we are, then we really are lying to ourselves. Convenience is an untruthful killer which is quietly engulfing the world. In the end I did allow two pieces of kit into my life – spring opening scissors and a buttonhook. My stumps would not open or close scissors easily and I cannot close a button that I cannot see. I can do the rest, but need the hook to close my collar. These are tools of necessity, not convenience. Just because you have a garage full of spanners does not mean that you need them all.

People can be honest in both a positive and negative way. If you believe you can do something, then you probably will, but if you believe that you can't, well you won't. Both statements are true and honest and helped me during my recovery. Sitting on the bedside one day I was convinced that I could walk, and I did. Had I sat there and thought it was the end and that all my attempts would be futile, then I wouldn't. Mountaineering is the same. Do you want to climb or not? Ok, so the weather has its part to play, but you need the will. I suppose the optimists and pessimists come in here. I sat in both camps for a long time swinging violently between the two, but I came out an optimist. It is incredible how much better you recover if you want to. Injuries mend quicker and you feel as if you are on top of the world, but I have lain in wards surrounded by pessimists. If you are badly injured and will never play football again don't fall into depression. Find something else and don't blinker your life with narrow-minded views. Go into coaching or helping in some way to stay involved. If you do the truth is with you.

Losing your fingers isn't good if you shoot, as I do. I had always been a very traditional man when it comes to guns and was determined not to change; yet I did. Why? Because every time I pulled the trigger a large part of my stump was ripped off and blood spewed out. I held out for grim death, but eventually I had to face facts. I changed guns and stopped the bleeding, but it was an expensive undertaking. Decisions can be expensive and that can put people off. "I'll have to give it up because I can't afford to change" is something I have heard time and time again. It's horrible when money gets in the way of a full recovery, but we all have to live within our means. We are showing further honesty if we do. In my case I thought it was worth the money for my fingers sake, and because I find peace when out in the fields.

My biggest decision came when I returned to climbing. I had been a good climber on rock and ice before McKinley, but now things had changed dramatically. Having no fingertips made rockwork, particularly granite a nightmare as my fingers bled on the hard stone. I couldn't grip the tiny handholds and stubbed my feet repeatedly. I tried all kinds of ideas, but none worked. Dejected I sat down one afternoon in Derbyshire and thought about what I was doing to myself. I couldn't push myself any harder than I was, and my confidence had been shattered. It just never came back to me after Alaska and I had to take the decision to loose the rock boots, go onto big clumpy mountaineering boots and give up the hard climbs. My hands and feet complained less on the easier grades and I scrambled more and more. Many people thought even that was good after what had happened to me, but I had a hard time coming to terms with it. Here was a decision I had been putting off for far too long, but had now put what was left of my foot down and stamped hard. Since then I haven't missed the hard climbing at all. I'm more than happy watching everyone else fight up the cliffs. Ice climbing hasn't been so bad for me, but I did realise early on that I was going to need professional help. Martin Moran and Chris Dale led the way in getting me back into winter climbing in both Scotland and the Alps. They helped me adapt my axes and have climbed some tremendous routes with me. I still have guided help to this day, but realise in all honesty it is what I need. Other people are out there to help in all walks of your life, and again I found it monetarily expensive, but can you put a price on rebuilding your life? Whatever it takes you must do everything you can to get back your life and independence. Take that away and you are not living, but existing.

I had never been a great runner, but found occasionally that it helped drain a stressful day away, and improve my fitness. I had run most evenings before Alaska carrying a 40lb rucksack to be as fit as possible for the climb. You need a great deal of spring in your step to run, and once my toes were gone, that spring disappeared. I tried new trainers and foot beds, but it was no good. The pain was just too much to bear and 10 minutes running made me hobble for the next few days. I just had to stop. Physical constraints at an early age are no fun at all, but when cornered you have little choice but to listen to your body. Mentally I faced the truth that I would walk or cycle from now on, and I have. I can run a few yards if I need to, but rarely do. My feet are too precious to me. I have a long life ahead of me (I hope) and need to keep them in tiptop shape. We all suffer some kind of change or loss in our lives, and deal with it as best as we can, but we must make sure that we are truthful to ourselves – inside and out.

Honesty in relationships was another matter. I found the physical things in my life easier to deal with, as being an engineer let me take a methodical approach, but the emotional aspects were something else. As before, everyone could see the physical changes, but no one could see the mental. I found it impossible to explain how I felt and went through nights of turmoil. I just couldn't perceive how any woman would ever want me in her life. It wasn't that I was being dishonest with her, but with myself. "Beauty is only skin deep" goes the saying, but I couldn't believe it. I lost the art of trying to meet someone, convinced that it was all over, and sat at the corner of the bar getting drunk before a long and lonely walk home. Salvation came unexpectedly. I found someone who took me for what I was and was bluntly honest with me. She shook me up and awakened feelings that I had suppressed for months, fearing they were gone forever. I have seen men who have suffered broken relationships live alone for the rest of their lives, convinced that they are spent. They live in fear of further rejection, but if they sat down and thought about it, they would see that opportunities are out there, if only they could be honest enough to face them. Don't try to perceive what others think. They will think whatever they want, whether you are an Adonis or a scarred veteran. It's what's inside that counts. Separate how you think you are seen, from how you are seen. One little word in that sentence makes all the difference – think. You may be a bit of a Mark 3 Cortina to look at, but boy, what a tuned engine there is under the bonnet!

The second most important people (after yourself) to be honest with are your family. I thought I was protecting mine from the reality of my situation by not being honest with them, but all I was doing was creating more problems that I was curing. I thought that delay was a good tactic in breaking news, but as I have written earlier in this chapter, it is not. I still feel ashamed at what I didn't tell them in the early days of my injuries, but at least after a great deal of consideration I did. Phrases such as "I'm fine, don't worry" come to mind. It was easy to deflect my honesty as we were on an international telephone line and not face to face. The modern world, with its mobile communications makes it easy to be dishonest or distant, particularly with the growth of text messaging. I admit it has its uses, but it is so detached from reality that people get sacked or dumped by text. Where's the honesty in that? That's just treating people as a convenience, not a person. Just think, are you helping, hurting or hindering the other person? If you can't say something face to face, then don't say it at all. Face them and they still may not like what you have to say, but will respect you for saying it. Treat them as a convenience, and one day they will return the favour.

The relationships within my family have changed out of all proportion. Being too protective can overtake common sense and make us feel claustrophobic. How many times have we heard "you will be careful won't you?" Do we purposefully go out into the world to enter harms way?" We know that people love us, but fear that they want to keep us close and wrap us in cotton wool all our lives. Read my chapter on Survival for more about this. We need to live as normal a life as possible and that includes risk. I am honest about facing risk, but family members struggle as they don't understand what I'm doing and why I'm doing it. It's hard writing about this, as few people will write honestly about the people close to them, but I feel that I must. Being a mountaineer is my calling in life. I'm honest enough to know that, understand what it has already done to me, and know that it can do it again. I hate dragging my family through all the emotional heartache when I go away, but they have to see me for who I am. The greatest man I have ever known is my father, and even this can make him cry. Real men do.

Do you find it hard being honest with those closest to you? Most people do because they fear what they will say or what their opinions are. As a child the worst thing that could happen was a telling off from your mum or dad, and in my experience that hasn't changed. You are always their son regardless of your age and they expect you to listen. Some can't believe that you have grown, believing you to still be in shorts and at primary school, but if they could be honest with themselves, they could see what they have created and moulded is not a boy, but a man. Of course this is easy to say here, but I wonder if we would be any different with our own children in years to come?

Having travelled so far for so many years I had made many friends and acquaintances. My address book is packed with people around the world, but how many of them are real friends? How many would offer you help in times of need? This subject has become one of the closest to my heart since that fateful day on McKinley.

Friends, or the reality of them was a hard lesson for me to learn. I foolishly believed many people I knew closely to be friends. How wrong I was. I found they viewed me as some sort of convenient acquaintance, happy to bask in my glory and drink my beer, but never returning the favour. I would hear about party's weeks after they passed to find that I "had been missed off the list by accident or "Sorry I'm sure we invited you, didn't we?" You don't mind occasional mistakes, but when it happens time and time again you get the message. I found a great deal of it was to do with the coupling thing. I was single a lot of the time and so I didn't make the seating arrangement fit the table. It is a sad reflection on society when single people are left out because of who sits opposite who. Do people think that we cannot fit in? Are we so low in their regards? Perhaps so. I'm not a man for confrontation, and so let these so called friends fall away from my life. They can go their own way living in a land of dinner parties and polite jokes whilst I live my life in the real world. If you are one of those people who cut out the single people, think about what you are doing. They are not a convenience that you can use as and when you wish. They are real people, with feelings and are just as much a person as the rest of you. It took me a long time to let some of them go, but I was honest to myself in doing so.

I found many people fear time. They must do as I got lots of "Haven't got the time for you Nigel". I make time for friends in need. I believe as a race we have to, as we cannot live alone forever. We have evolved differently than that. There is an old saying that "Whenever a friend talks to me I find whatever they say interesting". That is a great leveller and test for us all. Listen to the people around you. Some are out to use you, others to drain you, but some are friends who become close and stay with you. You may not see them for months, but as soon as you meet again it feels as though nothing has changed. These are the real people in your life. Treat them well and they will be with you forever.

Some people promise the earth and deliver little. This is another test of the people around you. How can you promise something that you do not give, and be truthful? Ok, so we all exaggerate at times, but there is a line to draw. I'm not saying that I'm perfect, but I do my utmost to do whatever I promise. This can be anything from housework to homework, but it matters not what it is. Living by your promises is what counts. I hope that I don't sound too righteous with what I'm saying, but I am passionate about this. We are surrounded by people who talk complete rubbish. All they have to do is say no and at least we know where we stand. If you can't do something then say it, don't promise you can. By saying yes we draw people into a false sense of security. It is hurtful when people basically lie to you in subtle ways. The truth can hurt, but reality often does.

It's true that I have changed, and so has the world around me. We have evolved together through life's changes and will continue to do so. I would never have been so passionate about many of the subjects I have written about if I hadn't been through all my injuries. Like many other people, I would have got on with life on a daily basis and cared little more about it. Speaking out about issues such as truth and honesty can make me unpopular, but I don't care. We don't live in a dream of fluffy clouds and angels singing. We live in a world of love, hate, fear and valour. Are we being truthful to ourselves by doing this? Does going onward forever with little direction matter, or is it a requirement to fulfilling our lives? I'm no philosopher, but I do know this. As a people we are surrounded by lies. "Never let the truth get in the way of a good story" is almost a motto for some people I know in the press. They surround our lives with headlines which burst out from newspaper stands. People's eyes widen when they read their sensational stories, but are they truthful. Are they even relevant? Many times they are not and people get hurt because of some editors swipe of the pen.

Television is filled with reality shows which burst with truth, but very little honesty. Take the numerous talent shows. The panel will give some very truthful remarks about your singing or dancing, and when it's bad some people take extreme offence, but if they had been honest to themselves in the first place they would not have been there anyway. This is what I'm talking about. If you have a talent then use it, but if you don't, then deal with it. Don't throw your teddy out of the pram if someone gives you the truth and you don't like it. I must sound like some real grumpy old man here, but not everyone can sing, dance, act or climb. Some are lucky enough just to do one thing in their life. The skill is finding what you are good at, and being honest enough to do it. If we all lived by this simple rule the world would be a better place and my Saturday night television viewing would be less painful.

So there you have it, my views on truth and honesty. You may not agree with my ideas, but think about your own. We all go through many experiences in our lives and as long as we are as truthful and honest as we can be then it will all work out well in the end.

CHAPTER 11

I grew up in the 1970's and I loved watching Starsky & Hutch. If you ever needed to know anything about chilling out, all you had to do was watch Huggy Bear. Here was a man who knew cool before the word was even invented. Nothing was a problem and everything seemed simple. If anything came to bother him he just shrugged his shoulders and let the tensions go. He's a man we all need to learn from, but where do we start?

Get your priorities right. The only way we can chill out is to find what's important and what's not. Who is involved and how it affects them. Some people suggest making a list of your priorities, and then crossing out the less important, to leave you with your true priorities. I find that if I prioritise and only do a bit at a time then I'm ok. It's so easy in this modern world to take too much on and then to hang onto it for grim death. Give some of it away if you can, and leave what's not important.

Take a career break. I found it a pivotal moment in my life which allowed me to relax beyond belief. That doesn't mean I was being lazy! Quite the opposite. I worked hard but on the things I wanted to do, not what others told me to do. I could travel, write, see old friends and allow life to catch up with me. I had been speeding ahead of it for too long. I wanted a change in career and the time allowed me to examine the options. It is financially difficult to take a year away from work and not all companies will allow it, but if you never ask, you'll never know.

If we chill out the effects can spread to others. My Mother went through hell when I was in hospital as she watched her only son suffering before her, but if I managed to relax a little she benefited. I'm not going to say she was as relaxed as me, but it was start. I worried about her constantly and that got me wound up inside, which wound her up and so it went on. As I hope you can see, there's no better time to start than right now. Don't let that spiral of worry get out of control. Start small and work up in stages, but don't expect to go from hyper to hypo in a day.

My Sister Amanda helped me through my injuries due to her caring abilities. She read to me, and protected me from the unscrupulous few that do wait in the wings. She was a little overprotective at times, but siblings usually are. One thing she could do was shave me. There's nothing worse in my opinion than lying in bed, clean and bathed, with new dressings on, but with a face like sandpaper. I felt dirty. I soon learned that nurses are not trained to shave men anymore and having hands like I did made it impossible for me to shave myself. With care and patience she scraped the sandpaper away and made me human again. I suppose it's like ladies doing their hair or make up. They don't feel dressed without it, and I don't feel happy unless I'm shaved. I certainly wouldn't have had anyone else putting a razor against my neck. She was my strength and my own private nursey. We had always been close and drew closer still through my experiences. I was lucky to have her by my side.

A problem shared is a problem halved. You can't chill unless you get things off your chest. I've always been a great talker with friends, and must have gone on and on about my life, my injuries and what was happening, but close friends soaked all this up and took it away for me. I've spent the years since taking it back, because as a friend that's what I do. Friendship has been, and always will be a two-way thing for me. I've always been a caring person inside, but usually cared more for others than myself. That can come with its downsides. I've had to learn to take better care of myself to allow me to chill. I couldn't go on forever doing things for everybody else and nothing for me. I would come home shattered every evening and begin work on my life until the wee small hours. I can't remember how much midnight oil I burned, but twenty-four hours a day never seemed enough. I am by no means master of all my time, but control it better now. If we can get this fundamental balance right then mentally and physically we have found the gateway to our health.

The physical health benefits of chilling out are huge. Who's read about stress and its connections with heart attacks? Ulcers? Bowel problems? The list goes on. The news seems abounded with them, but do we take any notice? I certainly didn't. For years I suffered the effects of stress, which got worse when I gained an office job. When I returned to work after thirteen months away I was put straight into the office. It was undergoing a massive change and was sinking under its own turmoil. It looked like I felt. I had always worked outside in the fresh air in rain or shine, and loved every minute. Driving a desk was the best thing for me at the time as I was still on crutches, but over the next few months my mind spiralled down and down. I escaped when I could, but the monotonous drive to the office and back every day began to take its toll. Recently I noticed what the daily commute can do to us. I visit London occasionally, and am always interested in people watching and particularly in their expressions. Why does no one smile on the tube? Blank, empty faces sit with headphones plugged in and go to and from work as if sleepwalking. Is this normal for humans? Perhaps being from a semi rural background has made me inept in my view, but the thousand of bodies' crammed day on day into the narrow carriages remind me of being back on the farm.

Back at work I craved the outdoor life, but opportunities were few and my injuries got in the way. A job isn't good just because it pays lots of money, or gives you health club membership. A job is only good if it gives you what you need. The market is a big place now and the days of forty years in the firm are fading fast. Get what suits you best, even if it's stacking shelves or picking fruit. We all need to get that work life balance right. In my experience companies talk a great deal about this, but seem loathed to put their money where their mouths are.

The amount of medication that I took has damaged my insides, and now they are my personal barometer. I know what stress will do if I don't deal with it, but it can be sometimes too easy to put things off until another day. Learning from this is important for me and it improves my day-to-day life. I find a good diet, and as little stress as possible a great benefit to me. I still like the beer and pies though...

There are also the mental health benefits. Some people are natural worriers and can't help themselves from getting carried away with the slightest thing. I've done it myself on many occasions in the past. Perspective is a great word here. Is whatever it is really worth all the worry? Just because you can't get mobile service doesn't means it's the end of the world. Try telling that to some people! I have travelled in many remote parts of our planet and seen people worried because there was no service, or no Internet café to plug their lives into. Does it really matter? Is it life and death? And anyway, whatever was wrong with postcards (even if they did get home six months after you did). I do sometimes worry about the digital world we live in. We are becoming dependant on it and more and more it takes over our lives. Here I am writing to you on a computer, e-mailing chapters and recharging my batteries, but you can't write a book on a typewriter anymore. The modern world wants it digital. Does surrounding ourselves with technology make our lives any easier or stress free? I would say not. If anything it is worse. These are the important questions we need to ask ourselves every day and I still do. After coming down from the mountain I realised that being close to death allows you to put things into perspective a little more. Reality really is real, and everything else is a bolt on extra. I don't recommend that you try this at home, but one of two of you will understand. Don't make mountains out of molehills, and yes, you can survive without an mp3!

It's all very easy being told what to do, but you have to go out there and do it. One of the hardest things I ever had to learn was the ability to say 'No'. Not in a cruel or vindictive way, but in such a fashion to make time for myself. People will always take advantage of you when you're kind, thoughtful and willing. Please don't stop being yourself, but take time out to stand back. No one can criticise you for that. Do a few nice things in that time, whether they be walking in the park, reading the paper or climbing a mountain. It's your time, so use it well. We don't often get a second chance in life. I'm very grateful for mine and intend to use it as best as I can. I teach children about my experiences, travel and spend time with my family. I'm by no means perfect, but I'm happy.

For years I have taken a few moments every morning to read. How do I ever get through a book like that you ask? The book is called ' Medications For Men Who Do Too Much' by Jonathon Lazear, and every page has a quote for the day, with an explanation on how it affects the busy man. This book was with me on McKinley and rescued from our last camp. Since then it has travelled the world in my kitbag, and is looking a little the worst for wear. It is in two pieces and held together with a rubber band, but I won't part with it. This little tatty pile of pages sets me up for the day ahead and allows me to reflect on what the next twenty-four hours will bring. There are many books like this, and perhaps for some they will help. Just a few moments in a morning can make all the difference.

Love Music! I spent years as a DJ and found that music could reflect and suit my mood. I don't DJ now, but music still plays a big part of my life. Sometimes I need a quiet classical to relax me after a hard day, other times I blow the roof off with Led Zeppelin and bounce off the walls of the house (not fun without toes). God knows what the neighbour think! I have some personal favourites, which are special to me, and I'm not going to go through them here, but hopefully everyone has some too. We can use them to help you relax, blow off steam or just down right enjoy ourselves. Music is so portable now that it can be a oasis in a noisy world, but I'm always careful not to hide behind it. I see so many people plugged into their earphones to shield themselves from the outside instead of embracing it.

The greatest thing I ever did to chill out was buying a VW Camper. She's a 1976 Bay Window and I love her. I sing, smile and wave to people when I'm out. It's just fantastic! I enter another world when I get inside her. She's mechanically simple and has better bodywork than me, although that's not too hard these days. Ok, so they can be temperamental and need lots of care and attention, but I would advise anyone suffering with stress to get one and head for the hills, beach or wherever is special to you. At least you can stay where you like and make the tea. They also make great hide aways and I regularly use mine as my office to get away from the phone calls and disturbances of modern life. Perhaps I'm trying to return to my childhood, after all when she was built I was seven years old, but she is a release for me. I had a happy childhood and perhaps the memories cushion the blows of this modern world.

I have learned my chilling from more than just Mr Huggy Bear. There are people in my life, like me, who have suffered and survived. We have helped each other through our problems and special friendships have grown. Richard has suffered chronic back problems for as long as I can remember. He squeaks and creaks occasionally, but does more in his life than most other people. We met years ago through Raleigh International and taught camp craft skills to hundreds of people. We thoroughly loved every minute, but he suffered. I can read peoples faces and I knew he was in pain, but he worked hard to impart his knowledge to the young faces around him whatever the cost. I was always impressed by his skills at teaching and the way he built a shelter, lit the fire and made cakes in a mud oven, even when in agony. We once had to drive him home with him laid out in the back of his estate car almost on a stretcher because he couldn't stand. It didn't stop him. People like this may be classed as 'Soldiering on", and Richard cannot leave his pain behind, much as I'm sure he would like to. It is part of his life, but he is a shining example of not giving in. His life has changed because of his back, but he always has time for a smile and some rather strange humour. We still occasionally teach together and still love every minute.

Chris was a guy I met whilst training for a trip into Guyana. He was a business coach and I found him fascinating, but it was three years after we first met that our friendship was finally bonded together. When I left hospital him and his wife helped me get away from home for a few days, to give both my parents and I a rest. We built my website, talked for hours and just had one hell of a good time. He insisted on pushing me around in my wheelchair and got very protective. As I recovered we kept in touch, still web building and talking. He was then diagnosed with Bowel Cancer. His life was then changed forever. I helped him as he had helped me, and to this day we still build websites and talk non-stop. It is our calling in life. He inspires me endlessly and has helped develop my speaking skills, which in turn has allowed me to unload my stresses. His ability to spread energy into people is incredible. People like him are rare.

Bob Forbes, where would I be without Bob Forbes? He recruited me into the Electricity Industry in 1985 and got me on an expedition to Chile with Raleigh International. It was there that my travelling bug was born. I have a great passion for cycling, and Bob was my chaperone on wheels once I had convinced the doctors I was ok to ride again. I stripped my bike down to every last nut, bolt and washer to teach my hands how to work, before spending hours on rollers pedalling away to loose weight and pump my blood around. I felt so much better for it, but got frustrated that I could not do more. After much badgering I eventually got out onto the road again. It was quite a shock cycling without much over the pedals and hardly a grasp on the brake levers, but with help I mastered it. Bob and I would tour Derbyshire and Nottinghamshire down quiet lanes with hardly a care. Bob then suffered a heart attack and so I returned the friendship and chaperoned him. I believe he scared the Therapists in hospital almost to death with his feats of fitness. There was no sitting around after surgery and he was soon back into long rides. Between us we make a fair cycling team, provided tea and cakes appears somewhere on the route. The speed is gone, but the enjoyment has improved.

You could draw a conclusion that all my friends have been through hardships and that I'm not the best person to be around. Am I a walking disaster area? No more than most I would say, but we all learn from others and there will be thousands of Richards, Chris's and Bob's out there. They learn from you as much as you learn from them.

Now I get onto what could be a tricky subject, Counselling and Psychotherapy. I was talking to someone recently about the amount of help people seem to need today. Lots of people need a shrink these days, or do they? Do they really need a professional to unload all their problems onto? Wouldn't a chat over a pint be enough? Real ale has certainly helped me. Richard kept me well supplied in hospital and every night I would drink a pint of the finest, but I'm not telling people to drink or become an alcoholics, quite the opposite. We let our inhibitions go after a couple of pints and release some of the Englishness many of us hide behind. I was offered counselling both in and out of hospital, and I accepted all the help I could get. There was just one problem – It wasn't regular, and in my opinion it needs to be. Support has to be constant otherwise you're wasting your time. Often I would be winding up to that Friday afternoon session with lots to say and find it would be cancelled, again and again. Others could only do a few sessions and then you had to move on. When you change councillors, you have to start your story all over again and that can be traumatic for some. The NHS offered help, but there was a six-month waiting list. Now I have a theory about this – in six months you have either cured yourself or topped yourself. It's not the best way of helping people. I felt in limbo, unable to move forward, so I turned to the private sector, but this didn't help, as we seemed to be going back to the start again and again, making little progress. Have I missed something Freud didn't? Does repeating yourself endlessly cure you? Eventually I found my own cure – Lecture and write about your problems. My English teacher said I was a good speaker (even though I was only 11 at the time), and so I set about bringing my story to life by speaking about it. Eight years have passed and I'm still speaking about it. I love talking to audiences and preparing the multitude of pictures and stories keeps me endlessly happy. Chris helped me no end with this and it was the best thing I ever did. I'm not going to say it would work for everyone, but try it sometime. The professionals didn't do much for me, but that doesn't mean they can't help thousands of others. If people need help they should be able to get it quickly and get on with living their lives.

I wrote about Richard and his back earlier in this chapter. Well I have a few problems in that department also. Being over six feet tall and digging up roads as a teenager has done its damage. I was ok when I worked outside, but when I was bolted to a desk the problems returned. I regularly suffered with lower back pain and have been known to roll out of bed and crawl down the stairs on all fours. Physio has helped, but a friend once introduced me to the Alexander Technique.

Besides the help it gives my back, it also it allowed me to empty my mind, if only for a few minutes. This clearing out sets me up for the day, and all the pressures of work and family can be blunted in minutes. No drugs, no Alcohol, just me and my mind. It is a simple technique requiring little more than a flat space to lie on and a book to lift your head. Others use Yoga or Meditation to similar effect. The important thing is to find whatever is the best for you and use it to your advantage.

Ghandi once said, "There is more to life than increasing its speed." I hope the words you have just read reflect that. If we insist on living in the fast lane all our lives, we will get to the finishing line quicker. Slow down, take in the view and wave to everyone as you go by. So then you VW driving, ale drinking, public speaking Huggy Bears. Go out there and chill!

CHAPTER 12
CONCLUSIONS

It sounds like I'm writing up an experiment for my 'O' level exams again. And my conclusion of the reaction is... But I'm not. This is much more serious than burning a bit of magnesium. I'm hoping that by now you have read about my experiences and the lessons I have learned from them. They were hard lessons but very important ones, not only for my life but also for the lives of others.

It's obvious that my life has changed and changed for the better. I listen to the people around me more, take in the information they have to share and digest it. Listening is something many people do badly as we have so much noise and distraction around us. Don't allow yourself to get distracted and remove the sound if you can. If someone is speaking then turn off the television or radio and listen. I have found that by listening I save time and effort, as I don't do things wrong and take in whatever it was in one go.

A good conversation is something we should embrace as we learn so much by speech and debate. I find that I listen better face-to-face than on a telephone or Internet connection because I feel at one with the speaker. They are before me in body, not hidden somewhere far away. Of course this cannot happen all the time but observing the body language and aura of the speaker conveys their message more than their voice.

We constantly hide behind technology, hoping it will save us from facing facts but it does not. How many times have we news reports of people being 'sacked by text message?' Is there any courage left in this world? We humans have evolved to speak to each other face to face and five million years of evolution can't be quickly overcome by one hundred years of technology. Only use technology where you have to, not because you feel like it.

I have learned much about medicine and frostbite since all this began but more importantly I have learned about myself. I am the datum point for everything in my life and I have found it important to know about that reference. It has allowed me to see the way in which my life is going and to make changes to the speed and direction of it. We may think we know where we are going but if we do not know where we have come from, then we have nothing to reference it against. I could never have believed this before I climbed Mt. McKinley but now I have realised it. Years in engineering should have made it obvious to me but I never even contemplated it. Everything I ever built had a reference and strong footings, otherwise it failed. My family are my footings and I am the reference. Think about your situation. Have you thought of yourself as a datum point which everything in your life revolves around?

I have tried to slow my pace of life and get more from the years I have ahead of me. I don't want to rush headlong into them hoping that all turns out well in the end. The increasing velocity of my life was affecting my health. Stress was wearing me down and forced me to consider a change. No job is worth a nervous breakdown. Believe me, health is more important that wealth. I have guided my thoughts in one direction and steered a new course. Difficult decisions have been taken and I'm sure more will come, but I feel confident that I can face them and make the decisions that I must. There is always the unexpected of course and nothing in life is simple or straightforward but I feel better equipped to face whatever crosses my path.

I have found that understanding pain has helped me live again. I think we must all feel some pain, both mental and physical to remind us what it feels like. That reality check gives us another reference in life to work against. It might sound a little masochistic I know but pain has been with us for thousands of years. It's just now that we mask it with drugs. I'm not saying we must undergo surgery and bite on a stick but if we forget what hurts and what doesn't, then I feel we are on a downward spiral to destroying one of life's most important and necessary experiences. This comes back to childhood as

I mentioned in an earlier chapter. If we don't allow children to get stung, bitten or bruised, then where will their reference point be? Mental pain makes deep and invisible scars but we need to learn lessons from them when we face it. If we don't learn then we stagnate.

A journalist once asked me if my accident had "closed any doors in my life". I replied "yes, but it has opened many more". How can I draw this conclusion? Simplicity itself – it's true. There are some physical things that I cannot do now but mentally I am alive with ideas and thoughts. I strive to improve my life and other peoples by my actions and never stop believing in myself. This has proved physically difficult at times, particularly when climbing but I find more and more things inspire me to succeed. I don't want to get stuck in a rut, because the only difference between that and a grave is the depth. I feel that we need to consistently challenge ourselves about our loves, lives and work. Nothing should just go in that same old direction. I have found that life's compass changes constantly and needs careful watching. I think we all need to see what doors we open and close in our lives and ask ourselves – do we need them all? Should we close one or two to prevent ourselves from being spread too thinly? I feel that for many people the answer should be yes. We are better concentrating on fewer things so that we do a better job and don't become a 'Jack of all trades and master of none'.

My injuries have changed my life. That much is obvious but I have to live with them and get on with life. No amount of wishing or whinging will change that. People will put up with you going on about your problems for a while, before their patience wears thin. Get what you need out of your system and move on. I know many people who, every time we meet go on and on about their problems. Some of them have not changed the record for five or six years. Ok, so I'm a listening ear, but we need to work out those problems and move forward. Don't wear your problems as proudly displayed medals. Use them as life learning experiences.

Suicide is painless, apparently. I wouldn't know because I'm still alive but it was something I seriously contemplated. Having sat in bed full of anaesthetic and pity I can assure you that it's not worth it. My experience was purely of a short-term problem that I struggled to handle but I seriously wanted to kill myself. This sounds easy to write about now but at the time I was in a real mess. I thank the Lord that I didn't do anything, as my life has been wonderful ever since. I have travelled across the world numerous times and met lots of new people. I do think the word 'suicide' is used too easily nowadays and banded about like some kind of joke. Believe me, it's not a subject to joke about. I have found that using words and language well in life makes a terrific difference to you and the people around you.

One thing I can tell you is this. I wish I hadn't had to suffer all the injury and heartache to learn what I have about myself. If only there had been another way to understand my life better without masses of surgery, pain and change. Sometimes we need an incident to kick us up the backside and make us change but surely we could do it another way? From personal experience I can honestly say this. Listen and learn from others like me who have been there and suffered. Believe me, I don't wish what happened to me on anyone else in this world, but if just one person can improve their life by reading about my experiences, I'll be a happier man. This is one of the major reasons that I sat down and wrote this book. Yes, it's a great adventure story but I hope it's more than that. I hope that it's a tale of overcoming serious injury and all the odds to live a wonderful and fulfilling life.

As men we suppress emotions well in the western world. Perhaps it's all a bit soft to show them but I have concluded that's all wrong. I wrote earlier about crying and believe in it to the last. Society seems to herd people into groups, some of which are tough, macho types. I have to ask the question "are they really?" Or are they completely lost in a world of peer pressure and talk? Are they 'trying to outdo the Jones?' or just undoing themselves. I'm sure it's the latter.

This is where I change the focus of this chapter from me to you. If you know someone who has undergone massive changes in their life then learn from them. If not, there are plenty of people out there speaking about their experiences. Go to a few lectures or read what they have written. Take in how their life has changed and try to understand their viewpoint. If you can, talk to them and allow yourself to listen to what they have to say without bias. Listen to yourself too. Listen to your feelings and emotions because only you can act on what they are saying. If you need to change then have the courage to do so. There is no point in lying to yourself for the rest of your life and regretting it at the end.

Believe in yourself. If you don't, then don't expect anyone else to. You won't get anywhere in life if you don't believe in what you are doing be it work, love or life.

Never give up. No matter what happens to you never give up. Many of the subjects I have written about all interlace and here belief and willpower come in. If you can put them together then you have a powerful arsenal at your disposal. A strong combination will see you through your darkest times and topics such as depression and suicide will be easier to deal with. Don't dismiss them as easy or you will be making a huge mistake. Don't become a robotic android with no emotion. Try to be a balanced being that faces life head on and takes the blows, but also the triumphs. We know this life is a rollercoaster ride but if it wasn't then it would be boring.

Of course it's easy for me to write these words and for you to read them. Acting on them, well guys, it's all up to you now...

Nigel in Sumatra, 2006

17051191R00094

Printed in Great Britain
by Amazon